The
Lynton & Barnstaple Railway

An Anthology

Compiled b
David Huds

GW00498414

Drawings b
Eric Leslie

THE OAKWOOD PRESS

© Oakwood Press, David Hudson and Eric Leslie 1995

British Library Cataloguing in Publication Data
A Record for this book is available from the British Library
ISBN 0 85361 485 7

Typeset by Oakwood Graphics.

Printed by Alpha Print (Oxford) Ltd, Witney, Oxon.

All rights reserved. No part of this book may be reproduced or transmitted in any form or by any means, electronic or mechanical, including photocopying, recording or by any information storage and retrieval system, without permission from the Publisher in writing.

Published by
The Oakwood Press
P.O. Box 122, Headington, Oxford OX3 8LU

Contents

Introduction 4

The Lynton & Barnstaple Railway, *by Philip Whitwell Wilson* 7

The Lynton & Barnstaple Railway, *from The Times* 13

Birmingham Daily Gazette 16

The Lynton & Barnstaple Railway, *from The Times* 16

The Railway Juggernaut, *from the Sheffield Independent* 17

Our Own Little Railway, *from the Pall Mall Gazette* 18

What I Heard Under the Table, *by Reg Jacobs* 21

Journal of a Disappointed Man, *by W.N.P. Barbellion* 23

Barnstaple to Lynton, *from the Red Guide* 25

Devon and Cornish Days, *by E.P. Leigh-Bennett* 27

The Golden Virgin, *by Henry Williamson* 29

On Foot in Devon, *by Henry Williamson* 31

Chillham, *by Mrs Millie Harding* 36

Childhood Memories, *by Leslie King* 37

How Dear is Life, *by Henry Williamson* 39

The Lynton Train, *by A. Fletcher* 46

Youthful Memories, *by Eric Shepherd* 47

A Schoolboy's Trip over the Lynton & Barnstaple Railway

    by C. Pennicott 51

Waterloo to Lynton - 1935, *by Hamilton Ellis* 55

The Children of Shallowford, *by Henry Williamson* 61

Lynton Railway Surprise, *from the Exeter Express & Echo* 64

Farewell to Lynton-Barnstaple Railway,

    from the Exeter Express & Echo 65

Letter to the Western Morning News, *by Invicta* 66

The Toy Railway's 'Goodbye', *from the Exeter Express & Echo* 67

Yeo - A Memory, *by Frank E. Box* 69

The Lynton & Barnstaple Railway, *by John W. Dorling* 75

Introduction

The Lynton & Barnstaple Railway stands alongside such lines as the Ffestiniog and the Darjeeling-Himalaya, as one of the world's most famous narrow gauge railways. Conceived at the end of the 19th century and running for nearly 20 miles through some of the finest North Devon countryside, it became a legend in its own short lifetime. Its gauge of only 2 ft enabled it to twist and turn in the hills, where the cost of a full-size line would have been prohibitive, and the little trains merged into the glorious scenery to become a holiday attraction in their own right.

Unfortunately, its trackbed cost far more to build than had been estimated, despite the narrow gauge, and on top of this crippling financial burden its birth coincided with the dawn of the motor age. By the 1920s road transport had begun to eat into the line's goods and passenger traffic, and as the receipts dwindled the standard of maintenance suffered. In 1923 it was purchased by the newly-formed Southern Railway, evidently as a public-spirited gesture. The new owners lavished money on it, even buying a new locomotive and eight goods vehicles, but the traffic continued to decline. It was the era of road improvements and the char-a-banc. In the Depression years of the 1930s this could not go on, and at the end of September 1935, a thousand people stood in the pouring rain at Barnstaple Town station to watch the last train come home.

The legality of the closure was questionable, but the Southern Railway countered the wave of local protest by ripping up several miles of track. With almost indecent haste they auctioned off the whole concern, four of the locomotives being sold for scrap for a total of £184! The bodies of nearly all the vehicles were removed so that their chassis could accompany the last surviving locomotive to a new life in Brazil. The delightful stations became private houses, an inn and a restaurant; the trackbed was gradually sold off to the neighbouring landowners; some of the bridges were blown up during World War II for demolition practice, and others have disappeared in the tide of post-war road improvements.

Nevertheless, the memory of the line is still green, and many of the old folk in the district speak of it with affection. There are no less than six books about it, one running to many editions, plus numerous magazine articles and countless models. Many of these models are mass-produced, such is the railway's popularity. Sixty years after it was so ruthlessly destroyed the views are as incomparable as ever, and even now much of the trackbed and many of the bridges are intact.

This anthology has been compiled from the many articles and books written about the railway during and after its lifetime. It is fitting that it should start with an interview with Sir George Newnes, the main energy and driving force behind the formation of the railway and Chairman of the railway company from 1895 until his death in 1910, and end with what is regarded by many as the 'obituary' article, which appeared in November 1935. The range of articles and extracts from other writings gives a flavour of the charm and uniqueness of the railway which even today still evokes a passion and a determination to prove that Paymaster Captain Woolf was right when, in 1935 on the morning after the closure of the line, he laid a wreath on the stop-block at Barnstaple Town station with the inscription: 'Perchance it is not dead, but sleepeth.'

We would like to thank the copyright owners of the material featured in this Anthology for permission to reproduce extracts from their books and journals. In particular, we would like to acknowledge the kindness and help given by Mrs Anne Williamson of the Henry Williamson Society, the Editors of the *Railway Magazine*, *The Times*, the *North Devon Journal*, the *Western Morning News* and the *Exeter Express and Echo*, and Ian Allan Ltd, Cassell plc, IPC Magazines Ltd, and the British Railways Board.

All the proceeds from the sales of this Anthology are being donated to the Lynton & Barnstaple Railway Association which aims to rebuild as much as possible of the Lynton & Barnstaple Railway.

David Hudson,   *Eric Leslie,*
Instow,   *Barnstaple,*
Devon.   *Devon.*

September 1995

"The Iron Pony"—journeying every day to the Switzerland of England."

The Lynton & Barnstaple Railway

Philip Whitwell Wilson

From time immemorial Devonshire, with its heathery moors, its deep, shady lanes, its wealth of blossom, and, above all, its delicious cream, has been at once the happy-hunting ground of the holiday-maker and the inspiration of the novelist and poet. Charles Kingsley, Marie Corelli, and the greatest of all interpreters of her scenery, Robert Blackmore, have each in their most famous works paid eloquent tribute to the fascinations of this romantic county, which rivals in its beauty and its literature the hills and dales of Westmoreland. Indeed, the Lake poet, Southey, was constrained to write of Lynmouth, the little port of Lynton, in North Devonshire: 'Two streams join at Lynmouth. Each of these flows through a combe rolling down over huge stones like a long waterfall; immediately at their junction they enter the sea, and the rivers and the sea make but one noise of uproar. Of these combes, the one is richly wooded, the other runs between two high, bare, stony hills. From the hill between the two (Summerhouse Hill) is a prospect most magnificent: on either hand combes, and the river before the village - the beautiful little village, which I am assured by one who is familiar with Switzerland resembles a Swiss village. This alone would constitute a view beautiful enough to repay the weariness of a long journey; but to complete it there is the blue and boundless sea, for the faint and feeble line of the Welsh coast is only to be seen if the day be perfectly clear.'

Moreover, the cottage at Lynmouth is still pointed out, half buried in leaf and flower, where Shelley lived and wrote. We may therefore assume that to the tourist - and in holiday times we are all of us tourists - the opening of the Lynton and Barnstaple Railway by Sir George and Lady Newnes on May 11th of this year is an event of the first importance.

In order that the information supplied in this article might come from headquarters, I took a convenient opportunity of chatting with Sir George Newnes, Bart., the Chairman of the Directors of the Lynton and Barnstaple railway, who, with his usual cordiality, supplied me with a great many interesting details. This is not the first time that Sir George has assisted in developing centres of fascinating and beautiful scenery. Only this year he presented to the town of Matlock the tramway which was founded and successfully maintained by his energy. Cliff railways situated at Clifton, Lynton and Bridgwater owe their origin to him, and during the past month he has successfully inaugurated a new Hydropathic at Bristol, and last, but not least, the railway we are considering.

'I believe,' Sir George began, 'that Lynton has for some time enjoyed the distinction of being the only place in England extensively visited by tourists, despite the fact that it is twenty miles from any railway station. Ilfracombe to the west, Minehead to the east and Barnstaple to the south are situated at this distance, yet it has been the regular thing in July and August to see twenty or thirty coaches and *chars-a-bancs* from Ilfracombe crowd into Lynton between 11 and 12 o'clock in the morning, and the directors naturally regard this traffic as likely to be a considerable source of revenue to the new Company. Almost by the time these words are in print the iron horse - or perhaps I ought to say the iron pony - will be journeying every day to the Switzerland of England, so that

tourists from Ilfracombe will only have to ride by coach to Blackmoor, fully half the total distance being accomplished by rail.'
The total length of the new line is 19½ miles. The stations are located as follows:

Barnstaple, joint station with L&SWR*
Chelfham, at 4½ miles from Barnstaple
Bratton, at 8 miles from Barnstaple
Blackmoor, at 12 miles from Barnstaple
Wooda Bay, at 16 miles from Barnstaple
Lynton, at 19¼ miles from Barnstaple

* The GW through carriages to Ilfracombe call at this station.

Of these, Chelfham is chiefly important as the centre of a number of villages. Bratton is important on its own account, a large village being about half a mile from the station, while Blackmoor is situated at the junction of four crossroads leading respectively to Combe Martin, Barnstaple, Ilfracombe and South Molton. Wooda Bay will ultimately be the junction for a small watering-place of that name, which, with its new pier, may be said to be rapidly developing. The scenery at Wooda Bay is such as eventually to render it a probable rival to Lynton itself. A branch line of three miles in length is contemplated to open up this rising resort.
At Blackmoor commodious stables are being built, as it is hoped the coaches will not run on to Lynton after the railway is opened. The horses will thus be saved the heaviest portion of the road. Through fares from Ilfracombe to Lynton are under consideration. The times for the coaches are variable, and the timetables are yet published, but last year they usually left Ilfracombe at 9.30, arriving at Lynton by 12.30. They commenced the return journey at 5 o'clock, arriving at Ilfracombe again at 7.30. About half to three-quarters of an hour of the whole time of a single journey will be saved by the railway. The following suggested time-table, which is not yet definitely fixed, may be of interest:

DOWN	Mail				
	am	am	am	pm	pm
Barnstaple (dep)	6.24	8.46	11.30	3.45	5.24
Chelfham	6.47	9.09	11.52	4.08	5.47
Bratton	7.06	9.25	12.09	4.27	6.03
Blackmoor	7.31	9.50	12.31	4.49	6.28
Wooda Bay	7.55	10.11	12.53	5.10	6.49
Lynton	8.11	10.28	1.09	5.26	7.05

UP	Mixed				Mail
	am	am	pm	pm	pm
Lynton (dep)	6.03	9.10	1.50	3.25	5.45
Wooda Bay	6.21	9.20	2.08	3.43	6.03
Blackmoor	6.44	9.53	2.31	4.06	6.28
Bratton	7.09	10.15	2.53	4.31	6.50
Chelfham	7.26	10.29	3.08	4.46	7.05
Barnstaple	7.48	10.50	3.30	5.07	7.26

The through trains are not very convenient this month, but in July the South Western Railway and Great Western Railway times are altered, and when they quicken their services the Lynton and Barnstaple Railway will be able to improve its arrangements in accordance. The through trains to London at present are:

LSWR				GWR	
Waterloo (dep)	9.15	11.00		Paddington (dep)	9.00
Barnstaple (dep)	3.45	5.24		Barnstaple (dep)	3.45
Lynton (arr)	5.26	7.05		Lynton (arr)	5.26

Lynton (dep)	6.03	9.20	1.50	Lynton (dep)	6.03
Barnstaple (dep)	8.11	11.03	3.52	Barnstaple (dep)·	8.11
Waterloo (arr)	2.33	4.40	10.15	Paddington (arr)	2.35

The fares on the Lynton and Barnstaple railway are as follows: first-class, 2½d. mile single, 3¾d. mile return; third-class, 1d. mile single, 2d. mile return. These work out from Barnstaple to

	Bratton	*Blackmoor*	*Wooda Bay*	*Lynton*
1st. Single	1s. 8d.	2s. 6d.	3s. 4d.	4s. 2d.
1st. Return	2s. 6d.	3s. 9d.	5s. 0d.	6s. 3d.
3rd. Return	7½d.	1s. 0d.	1s. 4d.	1s. 7½d.
3rd. Return	1s. 3d.	2s. 0d.	2s. 8d.	3s. 3d.

Through tickets are issued from all the principal stations on the South Western Railway, and similar arrangements with the Great Western Railway, and probably other lines, are contemplated. Cheap local tickets are to be issued on market days.

To return to Sir George Newnes.

The London and South Western Railway and the Great Western Railway have been quick to recognise the importance of this fascinating little line. At the last general meeting of the former, the Chairman stated that the Board of Directors anticipated the success of the venture, and expected the new railway to prove a useful feeder to his own line. Indeed, the South Western has shown its appreciation of the Lynton and Barnstaple Railway by building a new station at Barnstaple Junction costing £6,000.*

Here we may note that the peculiar formation of the country explains why the Lynton district has hitherto been left severely alone by the larger railways. Mr Frank W. Chanter, the engineer of the line, who laid out the whole railway and had sole charge of its engineering details, and who has subsequently been appointed manager, has kindly furnished many of the details for this article. He says,

The country was a very difficult one. The line was obliged to be carried over the crest of the hill at Blackmoor and also at Wooda Bay, and many diversions were necessary to negotiate the numerous crossvalleys running into the valley which the line runs through. There is only one viaduct of any magnitude. The maximum gradient is 1 in 50

* Did Sir George mean Barnstaple Town station?

. . . The curves are, of course, numerous and sharp, though outside the stations we have none less than five chains radius. The great difficulty in laying out the line was that the rise up to the two summits was absolutely necessary, and the Company desired to limit the grade to 1 in 50 as a maximum, consequently very little latitude was available. The line mostly runs on the hillside, where the natural surface slope is as much as 1 in 2 or 1 in 3, and the numerous crossvalleys gave great trouble. The permanent-way consists of 40 lb. flat-bottomed steel rails laid on sleepers 4 ft. 6 in. long, and ballast as usual. The same dimensions of road are adopted as are in use on the Festiniog and the North Wales narrow-gauge lines. The line is fully equipped with signalling of the latest pattern by Messrs Evans, O'Donnell and Co., and is worked on the electric tablet system with Tyers' patent automatic tablet instruments.

The question of gauge to be adopted gave rise to a good deal of discussion. But Sir George Newnes and his co-directors, Mr Jeune, Mr Halliday and Mr Hewitt, insisted on the adoption of the narrow 1 ft 11½ in. gauge of the Festiniog Railway. On this point Sir George made the remark that the cost of such a scheme was far less than would have been the case had the regular gauge of 4 ft 8½ in. been adopted. 'It is,' he added, 'interesting, in view of this controversy, to notice that, so far as our experience goes at the present time, the carrying capacity of the new line is as great as if the normal gauge had been adopted. By an ingenious arrangement trucks from the South Western can be run onto narrow-gauge trucks of our own, so that the goods traffic is continuous.' A glance at the (rolling stock) . . . will show that the stability of the passenger carriages is assured by building them very low onto the wheels.

Sir George exhibited some justifiable pride in the rolling stock of the new railway. The carriages are 35 ft long and 6 ft wide, and are, with small variations, of three types: (1) Composite carriage, with two first and four third compartments, disposed as in ordinary carriages; (2) third-class carriages, with seven compartments each, to seat eight; some of these have the centre compartment left open for passengers to see the view, and some have a guard's compartment and brake; (3) observation or first-class saloon carriages, for summer use. The carriages weigh from 8 tons 10 cwt. to 9 tons each, and are fitted throughout with roller bearings to decrease the effort of starting and traction. They are built by the Bristol Wagon and Carriage Works Company, Lawrence Hill, Bristol, and are extremely well finished. There are no second-class carriages on this line. The first-class carriages are all thoroughly got up in the best style, and upholstered in blue cloth, with maroon-coloured leather in the smoking compartments. The seats are divided to seat three on each side, and luggage-nets are provided, also the usual complement of photographs, mirrors, etc. The ordinary third-class carriages have movable partitions that can be removed in summer so as to leave the carriages open right through.

With regard to the observation cars . . . Sir George remarked:

Inasmuch as the line runs over a mountainous and picturesque country, and considering that the greater portion of traffic will be in the summer-time, we have made a new departure in the institution of observation cars, so that, when the weather is favourable, passengers may sit outside, with uninterrupted views, while at the same time having access, in the case of need, to covered shelter.

The locomotive power is to be supplied by six-wheels coupled engines, very strongly built, by Messrs Manning, Wardle and Co., of Hunslet Engine Works, Leeds. Their weight when loaded is 22½ tons. The cylinders are 10½ in. diameter and 16 in. stroke. The coupled wheels are 2 ft 9 in. diameter. The rigid wheel-base is 6 ft. 6 in., and total wheel-base 17 ft 9 in. They are designed to run easily in a curve of three chains' radius. The capacity of the water tanks is 550 gallons. They are calculated to take a load of 50 tons up an incline of 1 in 50 at twenty miles an hour. Their speed on the level is not indicated, but the Company do not propose to run anywhere over twenty-five miles an hour.

The cost of the permanent-way, exclusive of the price of land, was £3,000. Sir George Newnes expressed himself somewhat sarcastically on the difficulties which landlords throw in the way of railway enterprise. 'In many instances,' he said, 'the price we have had to pay for land has been very heavy. According to the opinion of some people, it has been extortionate. Of course, we all know how land invariably depreciates in value as soon as it is opened up by a railway!'

In conclusion, it only remains to be said that the first turf was cut in September 1895, by Lady Newnes, so that when the line is opened on May 11th of this year it will have been less that two years constructing. Finally, the railway has done no harm to scenery in Lynton or near it. The last mile runs through a wood and is scarcely noticeable. As a rule the track runs in a cutting in the side of the hill. The Lynton Station is about 700 feet above the sea, and a new road is to be constructed up to it while the existing road is being improved.

[*The Railway Magazine*, Vol. 2, 1898.]

–"Curves, frequent and sharp, banks and cuttings numerous and heavy."

The Lynton and Barnstaple Railway

From a Correspondent

Within the next fortnight there is to be opened to the public a new and very interesting railway, the Lynton and Barnstaple. Though a small undertaking enough, as railways count smallness, with a capital of only about £100,000 and a length of under 20 miles, it deserves notice from more than one point of view. For one thing, Lynton has hitherto been singularly inaccessible. There is certainly no other place of the same importance in England distant 16 miles from its nearest station. For another thing, though the line is not technically a light railway, as it was constructed not under the Light Railways Act, but under its own private Act obtained from Parliament in the regular manner, for all practical purposes it is what would be called in any Continental country a light railway of superior description. Then, again, the history of the undertaking is a marked exception to the rule of small independent companies. The line was promoted by influential local men, its capital has been raised without difficulty and on satisfactory terms, and the construction has been promptly and energetically carried through under the direction of a capable and experienced engineer by a contractor, paid not in paper but hard cash, month by month, as the work proceeded. Such a railway can hardly fail to afford instruction to those who, in other parts of the country, are promoting or desiring to promote similar undertakings under the powers of the Light Railway Act.

The railway was constructed with a gauge of only two feet, the same as that of the Festiniog and the North Wales narrow-gauge lines. But these latter, though passenger traffic is now an important source of their revenue, were originally intended merely as mineral lines. The Lynton railway is primarily built for passengers, though from its wharves at Barnstaple it will no doubt carry a good deal of coal and lime and manures to the farmers along its road. The line starts from the existing passenger station of the South-Western Company, and before it gets out of the town crosses two streets on the level, but all the other roads in its course, and there are over 20 of them, are crossed by bridges in the orthodox manner. No sooner is it outside of the town than the railway commences to rise from the valley of the Yeo on a steady gradient of 1 in 50, till near Parracombe, whose precipitous and tortuous hill no one who has driven along the coach-road is likely to forget, it reaches an elevation of 1,000 feet. Thence it descends on the same gradient to a terminus just outside Lynton, on the face of the hill looking down into the valley of the West Lynn. Needless to say, in such a country the curves are frequent and sharp, and the banks and cuttings numerous and heavy. There is, moreover, one quite considerable viaduct 50 ft high and 100 yards long. Yet the total cost of the works, buildings - there are six stations, all of them substantial stone structures - and permanent way, well ballasted and laid with 42 lb. rails, is well under £60,000, or, say, £3,000 per mile. It must be confessed that the contractor has good grounds for saying that the transaction has not been a profitable one for him. It may be added that the purchase of the necessary land, excluding property acquired within the town limits of Barnstaple, cost over £1,000 a mile, inclusive, of course, of compensation for severance, but only including a *minimum* sum for legal expenses, as in almost every case the price was fixed by agreement.

English Switzerland.

LYNMOUTH.

LYN VALLEY HOTEL

The LARGEST FIRST-CLASS MODERN - FAMILY HOTEL IN LYNMOUTH. -

Electric Light and all Modern Improvements
Good Salmon and Trout Fishing. Bathing.

Officially appointed for R.A.C., A.A., A.C.U.

Garage.   Lock-up Compartments.

Mrs. CECIL BEVAN, Proprietress.

Tels.—"Bevan's Hotel, Lynmouth."   'Phone—46 Lynton.

Rolling stock, signalling and telegraphs have absorbed the bulk of the remaining capital.

Of signalling and telegraphs there is nothing to say, except that the line will be worked on the absolute block system by means of Tyer's Electric Tablets, and that, though the speed is to be limited to 20 miles an hour, the points are all locked and interlocked with the signals. The rolling stock consists of four engines - one of them, thanks to the engineering strike, has been ordered from America - with six-coupled driving wheels and a two-wheeled bogie at either end and a total weight of about 22 tons, and 16 ingeniously-planned bogie carriages, only about 18 inches narrower than ordinary main-line stock, and most of them having an open-air 'observation' compartment. There are also a number of goods trucks, some of them on four wheels and some on bogies, all of them, fitted with continuous vacuum brakes, so that they can be worked on passenger trains.

It is proposed at the outset to run five trains each way daily, each train consisting of four carriages, and so having accommodation for about 200 passengers. Not that 200 passengers per train are likely to present themselves in ordinary circumstances; but an average of even 30 third-class passengers per train with a moderate allowance for goods and parcel and mail traffic would yield a revenue of 3s. 4d. per train mile, or, in other words, £10 per mile of line per week. It can hardly be unreasonable to expect this as a *minimum* when the Festiniog Railway earns £25, lines like the Highland and Cambrian earn about £20, while £10 is obtained even in the remote wilds of Cardigan by the Manchester and Milford Company. The really important question is what the working expenses will amount to. If, by the exercise of the same intelligent and careful economy which has been shown in the construction of the line, they can be kept down to £5 per mile per week, the company will do exceedingly well and be able to pay over 5 per cent on its ordinary shares. Of course, the great companies with their large ideas would scoff at any such thrift as out of the question, but seeing that on the Continent light railways are run for hardly more that half this money, while even in the United Kingdom at least one energetically-managed narrow-gauge line, the Derry and Lough Swilly, which like the Lynton Railway, is fortunately free from the incubus of a Government guarantee, manages only to spend £5 10s. in earning £11, there is really no reason why the thing should not be done. That some such result may be obtained is much to be desired, not only in the interest of the enterprising promoters of the Lynton Railway, but in that of the public at large. For that cheap secondary railways are wanted in many parts of the country is generally admitted; and that the well-meant attempt of Parliament to encourage their construction by microscopic grants from public funds is not likely to be of much assistance has already become plain. Rather has the remote prospect of a Treasury subsidy acted like the sporadic workmen's dwellings erected by the London County Council in scaring away from the field the independent promoter. Nothing could be better calculated to entice him back again than a 5 or 6 per cent dividend earned and paid by the Lynton and Barnstaple Railway.

[*The Times*, Thursday April 28th, 1898.]

The Birmingham Daily Gazette

The more or less reasonable opposition which has been urged against the Lynton and Barnstaple Railway has been fruitless in results. To-day the line will be opened by Sir George Newnes, and a most delightful district of Devonshire made more accessible to the public. The railway is little over nineteen miles in length, and has cost about £57,000. Fears have been expressed that it will desecrate the beauties of Exmoor, and let loose a flood of uncultured trippers on one of the loveliest portions of Exmoor. The desecration cannot be admitted, for the gauge of the line, which is only 2 ft, is too narrow to interfere with the landscape any more than would an ordinary pathway. As for the trippers, we profess no admiration for the unuttered doctrine that natural beauties are among the privileges of class; and the contention that the advent of the lowly excursionist will lead to vulgarisation betrays a selfishness entirely unwarranted and unjust.

[The *Birmingham Daily Gazette*, 11th May, 1898.]

The Lynton and Barnstaple Railway

From a Correspondent

The formal opening of the Lynton and Barnstaple Railway took place yesterday. Barnstaple was gaily decorated, and the Mayor and corporation walked in procession to the new station at the Barnstaple end of the line. They were received by Sir George Newnes, the Chairman, and the other Directors of the company, to whom an address of congratulation was presented by the corporation. Subsequently the directors and numerous guests proceeded to Lynton by train. Another address was presented at Bratton Fleming, one of the villages on the route, and at Lynton there was the presentation of an address by the inhabitants. Lady Newnes formally opened the railway by severing a ribbon which was drawn across the entrance to the station. A procession took place from the station to the Valley of Rocks Hotel, where luncheon was served. Subsequently Mrs E.B. Jeune laid the foundation-stone of the municipal buildings which Sir George Newnes is presenting to the town, and the day's proceedings closed with a display of fireworks.

[*The Times*, Thursday 12th May, 1898.]

The Railway Juggernaut

Sheffield Independent

The steam engine has already trampled much of what is most beautiful in English scenery under its wheels; but it has seldom selected a daintier victim than Lynton, the loveliest spot in Devonshire, and one of the loveliest in England. Today there will be opened the Barnstaple and Lynton Railway; and Lynton, with its fair companion Lynmouth, will become the prey of the cheap tripper and of the man who does not care to take trouble in pursuit of beauty. Until to-day the twin villages, one of them cresting the cliff and the other nestling at the foot of it, have had the inestimable advantage of being several miles from anywhere; but now they may be reached by anybody without further expenditure of time and energy than that required by a railway journey. We do not refuse to recognise the usefulness of railways in providing means of access to places of beauty, especially when they thereby provide a new lung to a great city. The Dore and Chinley line, for example, has been of high benefit to Sheffield and Manchester; and if it has not improved one or two places along the route, it has at any rate made a valuable contribution to the general health, and has encouraged exploration of more remote points in the district. But the opening of a railway between Barnstaple and Lynton is excusable on none of these grounds. Lynton is remote from any great centre of population; it is a beauty-spot pure and simple, and if one does not care to take some trouble in getting there he ought not to go there at all. If Lynton is to be sacrificed, what locality is safe? The lover of exercise, fresh air, and fine scenery will soon have no region he can call absolutely his own. The very mountains of England may soon become no better than the hills of the Rhine - many of them adorned with rack-and-pinion railway, a restaurant and a promenade. Some may rejoice that Lynton is delivered over to the clutches of the steam monster; but there are a select few who will mourn, and mourn with reason.

[The *Sheffield Independent*, 11th May, 1898.]

"Lew" at Barnstaple fair.

17

Our Own Little Railway

When we first began to 'move' in Lynton and Lynmouth, about the year when the 'Lorna Doone' coach commenced running daily, in summer, between Minehead and Lynton, we were a very primitive people, and our primitiveness, especially as regards our distance of nineteen miles from the nearest railway station, fascinated our few summer visitors, among whom were artists, literary men, two or three actors, some fishermen and a sprinkling of hunting men, some single, others with families, all forming a sociable community. To them the long drive by coach or carriage over the purple moorland from Minehead, or by the picturesque though less wild route from Barnstaple to Lynton was inducement rather than the contrary. Our visitors of those days spent money freely for the keep of man and beast, and stayed with us for weeks or months at a time. Although visitors, tourists and coaches were gradually multiplying, we smiled, in the 'eighties, at the wild talk of some of our younger men of the possibilities of a railway from Barnstaple to Blackmoor Gate, about eight miles from Lynton.

But, collectively speaking, we were ambitious. and a little ashamed of our simplicity. Our local tradesfolk and hotelkeepers began to make money and go away 'for a change' in the winter. They came back from places like Torquay, Bournemouth and Brighton with new clothes and new ideas. In due course the rough Lynmouth beach, with its huge rocks on the west of the old pier and light-tower, which have figured in numberless Royal Academy Exhibitions, was covered with an esplanade. This was soon knocked to pieces by the winter seas, but was subsequently restored on a firmer basis. A *funiculaire* lift railway was then put up, a cruel gash being made on the side of the hill for the purpose, to facilitate transit between Lynmouth at the bottom of the hill and Lynton on the top. Lynmouth village, which many artists maintain is, or at any rate has been, the most picturesque in England, with its thatched roofs and whitewashed walls, its gurgling river, and the valley of the Lyn in the distance, is threatened with transformation into a state of unsightly villa-ny; Lynton, the outward charm of which lay in the irregularity of the houses, has now its 'street' of small dwellings of stereotyped pattern, and the centuries-old church is almost smothered by an over-towering hotel at its very gate. Then wise men - men who some of us thought wise - came from the East, business and professional men from London, and pitied and patronised us of the West and advised us. Some of them would probably, if they could, have surmounted Castle Rock with a dancing booth, made a race-course of the Valley of Rocks, and put up a gin-Palace on the Foreland.

One wiser than the rest - perhaps wiser now than then - said we must have a railway, and the most headstrong among us echoed. 'We must.' The simplest way to get one was obviously through one of two the companies running into Barnstaple. Each of them, the Great Western and the South Western, was approached in turn, but - by mutual agreement, it is said - they held aloof, preferring to leave the financing of such a venturesome undertaking to amateurs. There was nothing left but, as our wise friends told us, to make the railway ourselves - and our fortunes at the same time. Apart from a splendid dividend - we were told how much - the value of property and trade would rise rapidly. A London barrister, a local resident who had run a sheep farm in

Australia, and a local shopkeeper who had lived all of his life nineteen miles from the a railway, were the moving spirits of the directorate. Money flowed in from all local quarters - from certain of the hotel proprietors, nearly all the tradesmen, from farmers and working men, several of the latter investing the savings of years in the enterprise. It was a great day of hopefulness and rejoicing when the first sod was turned, and even a greater day when the first train left Lynton for Barnstaple three years ago. A railway of our own! We were doing what two great railway companies had been afraid to do because they did not know as much about it as we did.

But what a day of realisation, of reckoning and humiliation, when the Chairman presented the Board's last half-Yearly report in the real town hall which is Lynton's latest joy. What a sad story of unforeseen expenditure, inadequate and decreasing passenger traffic, of a dividend-less past and immediate future - of cash assets little more than sufficient to repair a locomotive! And the Places for which the railway was to do so much have little to show by way of compensation. More people have come into Lynton, but mostly day trippers, who have revolutionised the character of the district. We who threw cold water on the railway scheme and other 'improvements', and were called 'old women' for our pains, rejoice, not because our incautious neighbours have sown in order that the shareholders of another railway may reap - it is more than probable the one of the trunk lines will, at its own price, buy up our very own little railway before long - but that the local epidemic of 'improving' has received a timely check.

The moral of this story is two-fold. In hastily striving to make new acquaintances one may lose old friends. Running a railway is an expensive game for amateurs.

[*Pall Mall Gazette*, 1901.]

Puff, puff, puff went the tiny engine,
and pull, pull ·······

What I Heard under the Table

Reg Jacobs

It must have been about 1903 or 1904. I was playing indoors as I expect the weather was bad or something, but the lady from next door was talking to mother about a Fairyland, and this caught my attention. So I stopped playing with stupid toys and listened. And this is what I heard, or as near as I can remember.

We went across London as usual on the horse bus and caught the train from Waterloo station, which was all quite normal. But when we got to the second station at Barnstaple, I think it was called the Town station, we got the shock of our lives. We asked the porter for the train to Lynton and he pointed to a tiny toy train on the other side of the platform and said. 'That's it. And you'd better hurry as it's about to leave.' Now, for the first time, we understood why we had been told we were going to Fairyland. None could have imagined anything better·for that journey.

The tiny engine was puffing away, and we had to stoop to get into the carriage. We felt quite sure that we were in a dream. The whistle blew, and the lovely tiny toy engine slowly started to take us along the very narrow track to our dream land. We were really on our way.

First it went along the side of a lovely river bank with sailing boats and all other kinds of boats and fishing nets drying in the wind. Then, believe it or not, it went straight across a roadway with lots of people and children waving at us from the other side of a white gate. Then past another river bank and still another roadway, and, this time, not only people but lots of horses and carts waiting for us to cross the road.

Puff, puff, puff went the tiny engine, and pull, pull, pull, we could feel as the seat we were sitting on tried to 'push' us forward all the time.

And what was that lovely music? You could not describe it. All the way down from London we had heard the wheels over the joints, but this was different. It was a soft and joyful music, which seemed to go up and down all the time. Then we saw what caused it. It was when the train - could it possibly be simply called a train? - went past the little banks on either side of the track, on which were growing flowers that none of us had ever seen before. You could almost reach the flowers with your hand. Then the bank would drop away and the lovely countryside with its fields and flowers and animals and so many beautiful things to see made the 'chatter' of the wheels seem to fade away and grow softer for a little while.

How we hoped that this journey in such glorious surroundings would go on and on, perhaps for ever. But no. Suddenly, and to our complete consternation, we went right up into the sky. We could hear the wheels no longer. The puff, puff seemed to fade away. Surely we were not really going to a kind of heavenly place? A rush to the windows made us realise, perhaps with some little relief, that we were crossing a very high bridge and we could see the people a long way below us. I have since been told that this was a viaduct and not a bridge. However, this beautiful little railway seemed to have just about everything, including stations with quaint sounding names - Snapper, Bratton, Blackmoor, Parracombe and Woody Bay - at which everyone seemed to know each other.

Then at last, and that 'at last' is one of regret because none could ever wish such a lovely ride to end, we arrived at Lynton station amid tremendous excitement. We heard. 'All change', and so the first part of our journey to Fairyland had ended.

But, truly had it? What was that lovely country just over the valley, with tiny people walking about? Over the masts of the sailing ships, surely that could not be England, with its twinkling lights and lovely white cliffs?

Seeing a man with a horse and trap, we asked him if he could take us to Fairyland.

'Oh. I expect you mean Lynmouth', he said. 'Yes, of course. And away we went down a long and very steep hill, and ended at Lynton. He told us that we had a longer and steeper hill to go down yet. He had to place some kind of pan under one of the rear wheels to help the horse hold the trap from running away.

Finally we arrived, and were just in time to see that beautiful sun slinking into the water, surely it could not be the same sun that everyone sees every day? Hundreds of tiny lanterns with glass bowls of all different colours were lit up. We had heard of the electric light, but this was the first time we had seen it. We walked along a little further and saw a tiny harbour with lots of boats. There was a grand and fine lifeboat, all lit up and with the crew sitting and holding up the oars, so that pictures could be taken of them with the sunset in the background.

Finally, after we had taken our fill of all the loveliness, we went to the house where we were to stay, but how could one sleep with our minds so full of all the beautiful sights?

It was another seven years before I made a return visit. It was not by train, but on a motor cycle. I still regret the omission to-day as the train no longer runs. I made a promise that one day I would come to live in this lovely place.*

[*Lynton & Barnstaple Railway Magazine, No. 2, 1980.*]

---

* Mr Jacobs moved to Lynton in 1962 and became Mayor of the town in 1977.

Journal of a Disappointed Man

W.N.P. Barbellion
(Bruce Frederick Cummings)

Caught the afternoon train to C—, but unfortunately forgot to take with me either watch or tubes (for insects). So I applied to the station master, a youth of about eighteen, who is also signalman, porter, ticket-collector, and indeed very factotal - even to the extent of providing me with empty match boxes. I agreed with him to be called by three halloos from the viaduct before the evening train came in. Then I went up to the leat, set up my muslin net in it for insects floating down, and then went across to the stream and bathed. Afterwards, went back and boxed the insects caught, and returned to the little station, with its creepers on the walls and over the roof, all as delightfully quiet as ever, and the station youth as delightfully silly. Then the little train came around the bend of the line - green puffing engine and red coaches like a crawling caterpillar of gay colours.

[Journal of a Disappointed Man, 1919. Entry for 17th August, 1911.]

"In Summer, cars with open sides are provided."

Barnstaple to Lynton

Ward Lock's Red Guide

From Barnstaple the journey is . . . by the Lynton and Barnstaple Railway, popularly known as the 'Toy Railway', by reason of the narrow gauge - slightly under two feet - and the diminutive but powerful engines. The line is just over 19 miles in length. The Barnstaple terminus adjoins the Town station of the London and South Western Railway on the Ilfracombe branch, the same platform being common to both.

The line was opened in 1898, prior to which date Lynton and Lynmouth were only to be reached by coach. Although the gauge is so narrow, the carriages overhang the wheels considerably, and are quite roomy. The first-class carriages seat three, the third-class four passengers on each side. In summer cars with open sides are provided.

The scenery through which this miniature railway runs is magnificent; the little winding line strikes through some of the favourite haunts of the wild red deer of Exmoor, and it is not unusual for passengers to get a glimpse of stag-hounds in full cry at the heels of a 'warrantable deer'. In order to avoid the expense of tunnels, long embankments and bridges, the line was made to wind and twist, so that its course resembles that of a mountain torrent. At more than one point the turns are so sharp that even a short train may be on both sections of an 'S' curve simultaneously.

After running through the sylvan valley of the Yeo, passing Raleigh Park and woods on the left, a glimpse of Goodleigh church tower is obtained high up on the right. The station is Chelfham (pronounced Chilham), 4½ miles from Barnstaple. The platform is at a considerable height, and the view from it is very fine.

Just before entering the station the train steams over Chelfham Viaduct, carrying the line over Stoke Rivers valley, which branches off at a right angle from that of the Yeo. It is a graceful structure of eight spans, each 42 feet wide, rising 70 feet above the roadway. White bricks are used for the upper portion, and no disfigurement of the landscape is caused.

Leaving Chelfham, Youlston Park, high up on the left - a favourite harbouring-place for stags - comes into view. At this point the line is 100 feet above the old coach road, and the view from the carriage windows is very beautiful. Then comes Bratton Fleming station (7¼ miles from Barnstaple), which will itself repay inspection. The rustic arbour perched some way up the embankment, and approached by zigzag steps, is used as a waiting room; it is quite a picture of sylvan beauty. Soon after leaving Bratton the line runs in a perfect horse-shoe on a bank which practically closes in the Bratton Valley. The opening seen in the bank, spanned by a bridge, was made in order to give the wild deer a chance of escape when pursued by huntsmen.

A considerable altitude is reached in the neighbourhood of Blackmoor Gate station, and the two hills near Combe Martin known as Great and Little Hangman stand up boldly against the sky, with the blue sea beyond, the Welsh coast being visible on the far side of the Bristol Channel. Just before reaching the station slate quarries are noticed, discovered in 1904 when excavations were being made in connection with the Ilfracombe water supply. They are no longer worked, the slate being of inferior quality. At this point the water main supplying Ilfracombe passes under the line. The railway continues a sinuous course, half encircling the village of Parracombe, which lies in a pretty valley on the left. On the hill to the right is the old church of Parracombe, now used for service only once a year.

At Woody Bay, the station for Woody Bay, Heddon's Mouth and Hunter's Inn, the line reaches its highest point, 1,000 feet above sea-level. From here there is a drop of 200 feet to Lynton. The last few miles gives the visitor a delicious 'first-impression', for Countisbury Hill rises bluff and mountainous right in front; and the East and West Lyn valleys stretch far away on the right to the heathery slopes of Exmoor. Another curve of the line, and the Channel comes into view; then the train pulls up on top of a hill, 800 feet above the sea.

Carriages wait to take passengers down to Lynton or Lynmouth, and unless one has sent luggage in advance it is advisable to drive. Or the luggage may be taken to the top of the cliff railway and thence to Lynmouth.

For those who prefer to walk, a pleasant path affords an easy descent to Lynton. The distance is just over a quarter of a mile. Round by the road it is a mile to Lynton and 1¼ miles to Lynmouth.

'Bus and Carriage Fares from Station: To Lynton by 'bus'. 6d. each person, 1s. with luggage; to Lynton by carriage, 2s. 6d.; to Lynmouth by carriage, 3s. 6d.

[*Red Guide to Lynton & Lynmouth* (Ward Lock), 1923/24.]

Devon and Cornish Days

E.P. Leigh-Bennett

You will get to Barnstaple Town in time for an early cup of tea, which will be ready for you on the platform. You will be glad of this because you will have got out of your big corridor coach here, which has carried you smoothly all day, and tea is certainly indicated. There is a change of trains. A change of a most astonishing and amusing kind. Sitting complacently at the opposite side of your platform, looking rather self-conscious because you are staring incredulously at it, is what appears to you a toy train. A tall man could lean his arms on the carriage tops. But it has a blustering little engine up in front which seems impatient to depart; and they are in fact busy round the little guard's van with your luggage. So you laugh and get into it.

The laughter, however, soon turns to voluble admiration which lasts for over an hour. In no other train have you ever been taken through such excitingly lovely country, or round such Swiss Alpine bends. It goes rather slowly with you, for which you are profoundly thankful, because if it rushed along, like its huge main line colleagues, you wouldn't be able to feast your eyes on the scenery, as you are doing. Delightful little stations it stops at, too - Snapper Halt, Chelfham, Bratton Fleming, Blackmoor, Parracombe Halt, Woody Bay. The bumptious little engine gives vent to a falsetto shriek of pride on approaching and leaving all of them. Perfect!

Meanwhile the scenery. Why hasn't somebody told you about it? The little foothills, copse covered; the panicky streams hurrying to catch the ebbing tide; two pale amber sheep dogs coercing a flock of harassed dun-coloured sheep in a red and green lane; mouse-coloured thatch crowning china-white cottage walls; an orange jumper hanging out of a window to dry. To the left the regal gesture of the Devon hills; to the right the rugged tableland of Exmoor, the home of the wild red deer. Suddenly, on a stream's bank, a little fence made of the back of iron bedsteads! This stream is within six feet of us, and the salmon know it well. We keep on going round corners. Now we are alongside a motor road - speed merchants smile at us and win; let them! - now we go slap through the middle of a wood, embroidered with rhododendrons and hyacinths. Now we skim round the fat side of a hill; a sheep dog gallops along the sleepers behind us, livid with expostulation at our trespass. Now comes the first hint of the sea; there is a look about these downs, an infallible sign. At one moment a chocolate-covered field is level with our eyes; the next we are searching the heart of a valley deep below. Woody Bay - 'tickets. please' - and then Lynton, all too soon, 700 feet above the sea.

[*Devon and Cornish Days*. Southern Railway.]

There is a change of trains.
A change of a most astonishing and amusing kind.....

SOUTHERN RAILWAY
WATERLOO to Lynton

BARNSTAPLE TOWN.

The Golden Virgin

Henry Williamson

The train rushed on under the sun shining down upon the green fields of Dorset, Somerset, and at last Devon. Here was the River Taw again, the thunder of carriages over iron bridges, with the brown shrunken waters of the river winding through the meadows, and then the marshes before Barnstaple. There they changed into the little light-gauge railway. Phillip* started off in the first-class coach, as befitted his status; the girls in the yellow wooden third-class coach. Then, after Snapper Halt, he joined the girls. At Chelfham they all went into the glass coach. At Blackmoor Gate he rode beside the driver, and worked the throttle to Wooda Bay station.† Then back into the glass coach, with its blue upholstery, for the arrival at Lynton. For an hour and a half the squat, tank-square engine with the brass funnel had puffed on and up, rising above oakwoods and steep coombe sides to the moor; now it was running down to its destination, the little wooden platform at the very end of the line . . .

[*The Golden Virgin* (Macdonald & Co.) 1957, reprinted 1984.]

---

* Lt. Phillip Maddison, who was wounded on the Somme in World War I, was sent to Lynton for convalescent leave. He was accompanied by his sister and cousin.
† Woody Bay station was originally known as 'Wooda Bay'.

"One Winter morning, we two stood on Barnstaple station, waiting to travel to Lynton by the quaint miniature railway"........

On Foot in Devon

Henry Williamson

Of a journey on a dwarf railroad to Lynton and environs thereof, and of local worthies whose habitations are or have been adjacent the metals; together with an *apologia et religio scripti*.

One winter morning we two stood on Barnstaple station, waiting to travel to Lynton by the quaint miniature railway, stamping our feet and watching the gulls as they screamed and wheeled about the froth of the tide. One would alight, then two or three together, a confusion of wings and webs and open yellow beaks.

The tide was ebbing and something was half-awash and caught in some buried roots of a tree; probably a dead salmon, dark brown, spawned out, one of hundreds which the floods were bringing down.

Steam was hissing out of the safety valve of the little Lynton engine, a curious flat structure of brass and green paint on wheels.

The engine driver smiled and wished us good morning. It was time to get aboard.

The gauge of the railway was less than a yard, and the carriages only held eight people, four a side. Some of them consisted of a single bench, holding but four, and into one of these we got.

The train started. It was good to be free. We took no thought of the morrow beyond what was in our haversacks. We wore light raincoats.

The train puffed over the level crossing and up the valley of the Yeo, gathering speed until with furious chuff-chuffing it reached its maximum of about 10 miles an hour.

The first halt, about three miles from the town, was called Snapper. The mist was clearing a little in the valley, and we could see the sloping fish-pass in the river, and two figures standing beside it watching the water.

At this season there would be few if any clean fish running up the river, and so the poachers - and, of course, they were poachers - would be looking out for the salmon kelts, or lean fish in poor condition which had spawned and which now were dropping back to clean, or renew, themselves in the sea.

The fish were surreptitiously sold in Barnstaple under the name of 'red hake'.

An old poacher once told me that he used to supply several of the local magistrates with clean-run fish. Once, when he was at his back door stealthily uncovering his basket, His Worship himself appeared; and having picked a nice maiden fish, His Worship told the poacher, half-humorously, half-seriously, that if he ever appeared before him the Bench would have to fine him. So an American judge in like circumstances would address a gangster supplying him with bootleg liquor.

We rubbed the steam off the windows and peered towards the river, but the figures stood still, watching the water. They must have been unemployed men.

Our train started again and we puffed up the valley, seeing the woods of scrub-oak which stretched up to the hill line. These woods renew themselves every quarter of a century; the crooked poles are cut for firing, and the oak sprouts from the stole, or raised root stock, which is left in the ground, after a score of years growth, the poles grow higher than a cottage, and anything from

"The new road runs beside the railway"...

4 to 8 inches thickness at the base.

The little saw mills at Chelfham (pronounced Chill-em) were working as we drew into the next station, which was built in the wood itself. The logs sawn from the poles are sold in Barnstaple and elsewhere for between 20s. and 30s. a ton; the trees themselves are purchased for £7 an acre. I don't know if the reader will be interested in these and similar odd scraps of information; but that's how I intend to write this book; and for those who don't care about following us, there's always a sharrabang round every corner of the main and minor roads. We're going by cliff paths, sheep and deer tracks, yes, and even rat-runs; we're going in the lowest pubs and by the highest tide-lines, too. To continue with facts: Between 50 and 70 tons of wood are yielded by an acre.

The mist was now rolling down the valley, and although we could not see any blue in the sky, we knew that by midday the sun would be shining with all the ardour that his low winter curve would give the earth.

The railway took a right-handed turn, half a mile past Chill'em, and we said good-bye to the stream whose alder-thicket banks led away up the valley to the sanctuary of forest and pond of Arlington Court. In this estate the wild red deer are unmolested, except by a stray deer-slayer; otters hunt for eels by daylight, the herons die of blind old age; foxes are never holloa-ed; hares lollop along before twilight, and the rabbits burrow into the lawns immediately around the house. The *chatelaine* generously allows visitors to wander over the grounds during certain seasons, which are indicated by printed notices by the various lodge gates.

So far the railway in the valley has followed a road very bumpy for motorists, but now the road begins to rise to the heights of Bratton Fleming. We in our curious carriage - I hope the Southern Railway people decide never to remodel these coaches - continue along the valley to the station half a mile below Bratton.

In the present age Bratton Fleming claims connexion with several figures in literature, journalism and drama - Mr P.G. Wodehouse; Mr Gerald Barry, founder and editor of *The Weekend Review*; Major Thomas Washington-Metcalfe, that writer of zestful adventure stories of a type rare in this age, combining a multiplicity of life against a psychological background of human endeavour reminding one of the Conradian imagination; and Miss Dorothy Bartlam, the film star.

Reader, the motor-coaches won't be starting yet; they hatch out with the blue-bottles and orange peel; but there's still time to catch the 'bus home. Read on if you so decide, but don't say you haven't been warned.

Our quaint little carriage was well-warmed by steam-heat, and as we climbed higher we were grateful for the warmth. Grass and thorn and bracken outside were white with hoar-frost. The engine was now puffing louder up the long incline to Blackmoor Gate, which was nearly 1,000 feet high.

To Blackmoor Gate the cattle of Exmoor and the north-west coast of Devon are driven and sold. Most of the farms in this county are now worked either as dairy or stock farms, and the farmers are not so hard-hit by the depression as they are in other parts of the country where corn is grown.

Farmers don't pay rates or taxes. All of them complain of the hard times, and yet it is noticeable that many of them own cars of the latest model. The farmers

"A photograph of me and my dog sitting on the engine

of the moor, of course, have the same struggle as they have always had, for their land is poor; but many of the stock or cattle farmers on the lower ground have comparatively easy existence in this age which sees the decline, through enormous taxation, of so many of the old landlords.

Nothing can ever take the old landlord's place; the State by taxation does not succeed him, but a score of little fellows get the land and exploit it for their own gain.

From Blackmoor Gate the line swings to the right to avoid the great dip which leads down into the village of Parracombe. Until the loop road was made the hill was considered dangerous for cyclists and motorists, for it went straight down to the village itself and there was a sharp right-handed turn at the bottom by a cottage. There was talk of widening the road and of doing away with some of the cottages, but fortunately it was decided to cut a new loop road to take the thousands of motor coaches which pass here every day in the summer.

The new road runs beside the railway, and joins the old road half a mile beyond and above Parracombe.

The village is a good one for the hiker. Let the motors grind themselves to death on the concrete loop in the distance, while for you, if you can find it, there is an inn where you may get what now-a-days is very rare - genuine home-brewed beer. This home-brew tastes of beer. It has none of that metallic bitter taste which the townsman is said to approve, and which is only saltpetre, fermented glucose, and other chemicals.

If you visit the inn in cold weather, when a fire is burning, get the poker red hot in the embers (avoiding tar-smoke) and plunge it into your beer. It's an old custom hereabouts.

There used to be another place in North Devon where one could get real ale, and that was in a one-man brewery in Barnstaple. A pin, or a 4½ gallon cask, cost 12s. Lovely stuff it was, a nutty flavour, yet not cloying. One could drink the whole pin in an evening without having that horrible morning taste on the tongue which the American dialect, with its present richness akin to that of the Elizabethan age, calls the 'hangover'. Good beer should have no hangover, either in the head or the palate.

But the world is full of bad beer, and it's too late to protest. The townsman likes the heavy immature adulterated stuff; and the one-man brewery is closed for lack of business.

The inn at Parracombe may have ceased to brew its own beer by now for all I know, although it is worth an exploration.

The next station is called Woody Bay. The old name for this was Wooda Bay, the 'a' being a diminutive: the bay of the little wood.

When this country began to open up for visitors, the local railway authorities considered that Wooda was perhaps a little too crude or too plain for the visitors, and so the old form was changed. The real old ale does not taste strong, but it gives you a grand feeling, like swift sunshine after dragging clouds and miserable rain. One day, perhaps, the chemicals in the breweries will be thrown away; and the 'y' will be knocked off this station board with a chisel and mallet; and the letter 'a' put back in its rightful place.

The run down into Lynton was interesting. One seemed to be leaning over the edge of a cliff. Big boulders in the stream far below, and white rushing water; the road winding wet and grey.

The engine ran as though tired, the effect of the coaches pushing the connecting rods into the pistons, for we were running downhill.

At last we got out, 800 feet above Lynmouth, and glad to be on our feet again. A photograph of me and my dog sitting on the engine, was taken; light was bad, otherwise the grins of the driver and fireman would be seen. Obligingly they backed the engine and coaches to help us get the best possible background.

['On Foot in Devon' (Alexander Maclehose), 1933.]

Chillham

Mrs Millie Harding

In my early teens I used to work in the big house in the woods above Chelfham station for the Chichester family. Sir Francis' Uncle George, and the 6.40 am mail train used to be the alarm clock for myself and two other girls to start the day. There were three of us to look after two people. In the evening someone always took the mail down to be posted just before the train arrived at the station at, I think, 7.20 pm. It was this short walk via a drive through the woods, lit by a 'bat' lantern, casting weird shadows in all directions, that scared me. For some strange reason, Mr Chichester would not allow his letters to be taken to the post box until the train was almost due in.

My real reason for writing is that I can remember Chelfham being called 'Chillham'; we locals always called it that. It was quite a surprise to me when I was able to read the sign post and discovered its real name. I lived in the village of Loxhore about 1½ miles away, veering off to the left on the way to Bratton Fleming. It was quite a walk to catch the train to go to Barnstaple. My late husband used to travel on it to the Barnstaple Grammar School.

We were all very sad to see the end of the Lynton and Barnstaple Railway, but of course for Loxhore a local bus service was just wonderful, scarely anyone had cars then . . .

[Letter to the *Lynton & Barnstaple Railway Magazine*, No. 26, Summer 1988.]

Childhood Memories

Leslie King
(As related by Mrs D.H. of Landkey)

During a Bank Holiday in 1934, when I was a young teenager, then living at Bishops Tawton, an exciting day out on the Lynton & Barnstaple Railway was planned by my parents. This was probably influenced by the fact that an uncle was a ganger on the little railway.

In company with three brothers and sisters we set out early one morning, travelling to Barnstaple in my father's cart drawn by two big horses. At the station we left the transport in the care of a local lad. We were greeted by the excitement of seeing and hearing a steaming and snorting 'Billy Puffer', seemingly impatient to pull a long row of small carriages along the shining ribbons of rail. The driver was Mr Nutt.

Many people were jostling around and about the interchange station, adjacent to the River Taw. A sea of cloth caps, a sprinkling of bowlers, and a flowery array of ladies' hats distinguished the passengers from the important-looking railway staff. After some confusion, all were seated in time, and with a high-pitched whistle or hoot as on a steam traction engine, the little engine bravely took the strain and hurtled us all away into the great unknown at about 10 miles an hour.

All, or most, heads were turned to look out of the windows on both sides, for there were many new views not to be missed. Where the Civic Centre building now stands with all its staring windows, the train rounded a sweeping curve alongside the smaller River Yeo, which enters the Taw a few hundred yards west of the station. This area used to be known as 'Monkey Island', probably because monkey trees were planted there. High tides caused annual flooding in this part of the town, owing to the proximity of the two rivers.

The journey continued into the countryside towards the hills and combes where our objective lay - the small town of Lynton, from where the smaller Lynmouth is reached by a cliffside lift, operated by the weight of water in and out of special tanks, down to sea level. On this bright and sunny day - it always shone in those far-off summer days - the journey was made memorable by the passing parade of rhododendrons and numerous wild flowers such as foxgloves, which abound in this county. The even wilder sheep and cattle were spurred by our engine's voice to remove themselves from the line, where the fences had failed to deter them.

Deer at Chelfham near the viaduct caused great interest, as did thoughts of our train falling onto the houses and road below the viaduct. A few mothers' hands were being held tightly at that point. Then again, at Blackmoor, deer were running a race with us - they won! Having survived the ride over numerous road and river bridges, enlivened by snaking our way around impossible curves and straining up the gradients we arrived at Lynton station where the triumphant engine panted with relief and was ready to be fed and watered.

So then we wended our various ways to find a good picnic spot, until we were ready to reverse the proceedings. Then home, covered in smuts and jam, to dream of the day out.

My mother was at the Grand Opening of the railway in 1898, and with grandparents and nine children rode to Blackmoor. With a heavy load this was a slow ride, giving some passengers time to alight and pick flowers, catching up the train afterwards. Apparently, on some journeys to Lynton another engine had to be sent from Barnstaple as a banker, such was the unexpected load. Other times might see two engines up front. It is local history that on another journey Lord Chichester of Arlington Court missed the train from Barnstaple. He promptly hired a horse and galloped off to catch up with the train, which he did somewhere between Chelfham and Parracombe.

I was at Barnstaple station to see the very last train in 1935. The overall impression was of sadness.

Sadly, owing to 'business' reasons, such trips are no more, but perhaps with all the problems solved we may be able to re-live our past excitements in the future.

[*Lynton & Barnstaple Railway Magazine*, No. 19, Spring 1986.]

How Dear is Life

Henry Williamson

The river widened into sudden sunshine. It moved slowly, with some scum on it, under oakwoods which came down to its steep sides, as muddy as the reaches of the Thames when the tide is out. Could they be near the sea? He leaned out of the window, and saw, faintly under the spiky western sun, a pale length of sand with heat-hazed hills beyond. This must be Barnstaple! He put bag and rod on the seat before him, alert with excitement.

Aunt Theodora had written that he must stay in the train until the second stop, at the town station; and then change to the small-gauge Lynton train he would see awaiting the London train on the opposite platform. It would take almost two hours to Lynton, but the country was very beautiful, she said. Sylvia would meet him at Lynton station, if she was not able to come herself and bring him down to the cottage.

He got into the miniature Lynton train. The engine looked like a green oblong tank, with a red cow-catcher in front. It had a big polished brass dome like an immense fireman's helmet rising out of the middle of the tank. There were only three carriages, one of them almost made of glass, the first-class one. He got into the third, and stared about him, at the swans in the river, wooden ships moored at the quay on one side, and the number of traps and carts drawn by horses on the road seen through the opposite window. There was only one other person in his carriage, an old farmer with mutton-chop whiskers and a square sort of bowler hat in his hand.

At last the tiny engine gave a discordant shriek of its twin brass whistles, and with much chuffing, and rattling of the carriage, started off. By the rapid chuffing it seemed to be racing, until by comparison with the people and houses outside it was seen to be creeping. The longer it took the better. To ride in such a train was an advantage which he would like to go on for ever.

The engine puffed and huffed out of the town, and up a green valley with oakwoods on either side, and meadows thick with rushes, where sheep and red cattle grazed. It passed over very small bridges, and left whiffs of steam through cuttings like a story-book train. Once it stopped, for a bullock on the line. He saw large birds soaring in wide spirals far above a hill, and counted seven, one above the other, sailing serenely in the blue.

'Good lord!' he said to the bewhiskered farmer opposite, 'They must be buzzards!'

The farmer grinned, revealing brown stumps of teeth. 'Aiy', he said, 'they'm 'awks.'

'Aren't they rather rare?'

'Noomye!' shouted the farmer. 'Serredwads fessans us calls 'n.'

He wondered what this meant. It must be dialect. It seemed appropriate with the name of the little station, SNAPPER, where the farmer, who was almost as round as a barrel, and seemed to have some of the contents of one inside him, got out. Head out of the window, Phillip asked the guard what was the local name for buzzards.

Turning to the same farmer, the guard shouted, 'What be they birds up auver, Jem?'

'Aw, they'm 'awks, I reckon! Us calls'n serredwads fessans yurrabouts, midear, it ban't thik praper name, noomye, 'tes only what us calls'n yurrabouts like.'

'Oh, thank you', said Phillip, as puzzled as before, for he had not understood a word of it.

The safety valve of the engine was screeching with the head of steam got up for the long haul to the moor. The engine driver had blown his whistle, and the train had started off again, when Phillip heard shouting, and poking his head out of the window he saw the figure of a parson running and waving his black shovel hat. The train stopped with a jerk.

'Afternoon, Joe!' shouted the parson to the driver. 'Billy Chugg's bees have been playing again.' As he passed Phillip's window, he stopped and said, 'Hullo' I haven't seen you before, have I?' When Phillip replied that it was his first ride on the railway, the parson said, 'Get your things - no leave them where they are, they'll be quite safe - and come with me into the end coach. You'll get a much better perspective of the curves from the tail. There's a grand view of the Chill'em viaduct, in the declining sunlight. The infra rays reflect beautifully from the white Marland brick. Let me give you a hand with your bag.'

While the driver waited, Phillip transferred bag and rod to the end coach.

'Very few visitors know what to look for on this line,' the parson continued, seating himself opposite. The engine screeched once more; and making an enormous show of power and speed, rattled on slowly.

'Once over Collard Bridge the gradient rises one in fifty for the next eight miles', went on the parson, as he thrust a hand into a jacket pocket pulled out what looked like a pinch of dust, and threw it out of the window. Phillip wondered why he did not stand up and turn his pocket-lining out by the window, if he wanted to clean it out. Instead, the parson removed the dust pinch by pinch, throwing each little bit out of the window.

'You'll notice we ricochet from side to side from onwards. It's a bore, but not due to any intemperance on the part of the engine, but to the eccentricity of the landowner in not allowing the engineer to follow the best levels when the line was first surveyed.'

Having said this in his dry voice, the parson sprang from his seat to fling another pinch of dust out into the air. As the train rounded a long curve, he continued to throw out pinches.

'We go under the road in a minute, rocks in shadow. I must hold my fire.'

The noise of wheels echoed back from rocky walls of green with ferns.

'Now look out, dear boy and observe the effect of the declining sun on the brick of the Chill'em viaduct! *A rose-red city half as old as Time*, you know the allusion, no doubt. We have to put on all power here, to get up to Chill'em station.'

While speaking, the parson was collecting more dust meticulously from his pocket. Phillip wondered if he were throwing out seeds - as he had once done himself.

The train was climbing through the woods; and suddenly was upon a bridge of several arches, but much taller than those seen from the train to London Bridge. It was built of white brick apricot-yellow in the light of the westering

"It was a dream country, floating in sunshine".

sun.

'Some visitors object to the white bricks, they look too much like a London underground lavatory, they complain, but I tell 'em it's the clay of the country, from Dolton and Marland beyond Bideford. The materials of the country can't be wrong. We're seventy feet above the road, now. That's the view I wanted you to see.'

The hillside station was enwound along its margins with rambler roses, hollyhocks and sunflowers. Phillip saw the name was Chelfham. No one got out, no one got in. They seemed to be the only passengers in the train.

As they went on, the parson explained that he hoped to see in a year or two, upon the sides of the cutting, various flowers in bloom, including stocks, wallflowers, pansies, night primroses, and balsam. 'Good for bees', he said, 'as well as adding to the gaiety of nations. Don't you agree?'

'Yes, sir', said Phillip. 'I threw out some bluebell seeds last year on the Bermondsey Embankment, near London, but none have come up yet.'

'Good man', replied the parson. 'Good fellow. They will! You're on holiday from Town? Got your rod, I see. Nice length for the glen, for sideway casting under the bushes. Fish wet or dry? Hawthorn gets 'em this time of the year, dapped, when the water's gin clear. You fished the Lyn before?'

'No, sir, but my father has. Oh, by the way, I wonder if you can tell me the local name for a buzzard?'

'I don't know of any, unless it is 'hawk.'

'I heard someone just now calling them something like "serrards fessans", and have been wondering what that means.'

'Oh, I can answer that! Sir Edward's pheasants!' cried the parson. 'The woods are so poached by fellows coming out of Derby, this end of Barnstaple, that Sir Edward hasn't a bird left. So the hawks are, in effect, his only pheasants, I suppose. Well, I wish you a pleasant holiday. I get out here at Bratton. Good day to you!'

The parson got out among more roses and hollyhocks. 'Don't forget to try a hawthorn!' he called out, as he prepared to get into the dray waiting for him.

'Good day to you, sir!' cried Phillip, waving his straw hat out of the window.

His new friend had told him to look out for the four farms on the hillside - Knightacott, Narracott, Sprecott, and Hunnacott - and for the streams sometimes passing over the top of the engine and coaches by wooden aqueducts. Phillip looked for these, until the train had climbed away from the deep valley. From now on it ran through rocky cuttings and high embankments on which yellow furse bloomed, filling the carriage with its sweet smell. Bees wandered through the open window, like the butterflies of hours ago; long ago in the morning of the day whose eternity was now ending.

It was a dream country, floating on sunshine, the world lying far below. Were some of the shaggy men with dogs, drovers of cattle, descendants of the Doones? The train stopped at Blackmoor gate; in a drowse of steam he listened to strange words and voices of rough shaggy men with sticks in hand shouting at bullocks among barking shaggy dogs. All seemed to share one language. At last the stamping was finished, and with the cattle truck coupled, the train went on, crawling to Parracombe Halt. Thereafter views of the moor, purple above

"Yuffing Yeo was running down above the oakwoods
of the Lyn valley."...

the far smooth azure Severn Sea; then a louder chuffing of yuffing *Yeo*, or whatever the old engine was called, echoed from the trees of Wooda Bay - another name mentioned by Father, Little Wood Bay. They were now surely at the highest part of the moor. It was shimmering, with the shimmer of a bee's wing! Leaning out of the window, he gazed upon the calm grey-blue sea stretching to a layer of white bubbled clouds above a far land. Good lord, it must be Wales!

He had travelled a great distance to be within sight of Wales! He waved his arms, and jigged upon the carriage floor.

The last orange was eaten, the last glaze of the sun upon the sea was glimpsed, and then yuffing *Yeo* was running down above the oakwoods of the Lyn valley, to the terminus on the side of the hill above the town. Alas, the journey was over. He said goodbye to his carriage, and to the valiant little engine that had pulled him to his destination; and got out, to the melancholy belving of cattle behind - and saw he was the only passenger.

['How Dear is Life' (Macdonald & Co.), 1954.]

THE LYNTON TRAIN

Oh, little train to Lynton,
no more we see you glide,
Among the glades and valleys
and by the steep hillside.

~

The fairest sights in Devon
were from your windows seen
The moorland's purple heather,
blue sea, and woodland green.

~

And onward like a river
in motion winding slow
Through fairylands enchanted
thy course was wont to go.

~

Where still the hills and valleys
in sunshine and in rain
Will seem to wait for ever,
the coming of the train.

By A. FLETCHER

From North Devon Journal, September 1935.

Youthful Memories

Eric Shepherd

In the summer of 1935, as a very youthful railway enthusiast, I discovered that a narrow gauge railway existed in North Devon. After persuading my very kind parents that a holiday in Barnstaple would be excellent idea, we arrived there on Saturday, 31st August. The following day, after attending the evening service at the Methodist Church, we walked down to the Barnstaple Town station. At that time I had never seen a narrow gauge locomotive or railway, so the evening train from Lynton was awaited with considerable excitement. In a few minutes, the 7.52 pm came into sight, the locomotive being, I am almost sure, *Exe*, and I can still recall the moment as she came round the curve of North Walk in reverse and drew to a halt at the platform, immediately opposite where we were standing in the road outside the station railings. One of the crew came to change the lamps, remarking that the train had been full. Looking into the cab, I remember seeing the brass beading over the firebox gleaming in the fading evening light.

In those days, the Southern Railway issued area weekly season tickets, printed on thick green card, sized about 3½ inches by 2½ inches, with rounded corners. Centred at Barnstaple, one area covered the lines to Copplestone, Torrington, Ilfracombe and, of course, Lynton. All the station names were printed in capital letters, except Snapper, Parracombe and Caffyn's Halt, which were printed in letters of smaller print. The cost for an adult was 10s. 6d. (52½p). Mine was 5s. 3d. (26½p).

Having purchased three of these tickets, we had two return trips over the whole of the Lynton line, on the 3rd and 9th September, travelling out on the 10.15 am train. I cannot now remember the details of each individual trip, but I can recall that at least one of them was double headed, *Lyn* being one of the locomotives.

On the outward journey this train departed from Snapper Halt with considerable jerk, provoking comment from people in the next compartment. As the partitions did not reach up to the roof of the coach, it was not difficult to overhear the remarks. Throughout the journey it was frequently possible to see the locomotives nosing around the curves as the line twisted and turned along the hillsides.

Whilst at Chelfham, one of the engine crew walked past our carriage and was exhorted by a gentleman from the next compartment to 'stoke her up'. For his advice, he was invited onto the footplate, and rode, I think, as far as Bratton Fleming

We left Chelfham in a vast cloud of escaping steam and continued to climb up towards Blackmoor Gate. At times the speed to me seemed very slow, but I hadn't realised then that we had nearly 1,000 feet to climb before we reached Woody Bay Station. Bratton Fleming was very picturesque with its flowers, and another feature which I recall was the number of small aqueducts over the cuttings, presumably to carry the streams across the line. On the way out, Blackmoor Gate didn't seem to make much of an impression, but then followed the great embankment leading to Parracombe Halt, where we took water from the tank by the road bridge. At Woody Bay there were a number of wicker baskets on the platform, which for some reason I remember, but I cannot imagine why.

The run down to Lynton (did we stop at Caffyn's Halt or not?) followed, the only memory being another view of the front of the train on the curve at Dean Steep, and then we were there.

Each of the days was spent visiting both Lynton and Lynmouth, including a trip on the Cliff Railway, and on each occasion we returned to the station for the 6.07 pm return train.

The train from Barnstaple arrived at 5.55 pm and some newspapers were unloaded. There was time to examine one of the carriages with the unglazed compartment in the centre, before we were away, double headed on one trip with *Lew* piloting *Lyn*. The former came off at Blackmoor, the crew giving a cheery greeting as they passed on their way back to Lynton.

The rest of the journey was a delight, a fine summer evening with scores of rabbits in the lineside fields and the locomotives coasting the curving route towards Barnstaple.

Unlike some narrow gauge railways which mouldered into closure the Lynton line did not have a run-down appearance at the end, and I saw all the locomotives in steam during that week. It must be said, though, that the majority of passengers were holidaymakers.

Six years were to elapse before I visited Barnstaple again, and in October 1941 I took the 'bus to Lynton. Large sections of the railway's route were, of course, still visible from the road and at Skew Bridge, beyond Snapper Halt, the trackbed had already been filled in and the road alignment improved.

At Lynton station the locomotive shed, station nameboard and bay platform were visible, but the brick edge of the arrival platform had gone and the site of the arrival line was a garden.

A visit to Snapper Halt to see the coaches revealed that the one at the platform (SR No. 6991) had been shortened and the bogies and track removed. The other coach (SR No. 6993) was complete and still in Southern livery. The doors were not locked and all the internal fittings, including the cushions on the wooden 3rd class seats and the photographs in the 1st class, with its dark blue upholstery, were still present.

Two years later, whilst visiting Lapford, I went to Clannaborough Rectory at Copplestone and was allowed to examine coach No. 2 (SR No. 6992). It was in 'as purchased' condition, complete even to the wooden destination board on the exterior, but had been at least partially repainted. The occupier of the Rectory informed me that the coach had been purchased by a previous occupier, Mr R.C. Copleston, who had since moved to Lapford.

On the following day, 12th October 1943, I visited Mr Copleston, who received me very kindly, and showed me a photograph album of L&B pictures, including some of *Lew* on the demolition train. Also in the garden of his house was a seat from Blackmoor station and the nameboard from Snapper Halt.

As I wished to see what remained of the line away from the main road, I caught a 'bus to Blackmoor Gate on the 15th October, and walked along most of the trackbed down to Snapper Halt. Looking back now, I wonder why I wasn't charged with trespass, but luckily nobody objected to my trek.

My notes state that at Blackmoor Gate station, 'no ballast left, Lynton waiting room derelict. A nissen hut on Barnstaple platform and line.'

I joined the trackbed just on the Barnstaple side of the station, and after negotiating a demolished underbridge and overgrown cutting, passed under a bridge carrying the Loxhore road and entered a wet cutting crossed by an overbridge. Next came an embankment across a valley, with two bridges demolished on the far side (this must be the portion now under Wistlandpound Reservoir) following by 'a well-preserved section with ballast in good order, then not so good past Hunnacott.' Here was an aqueduct across the route, and after Sprecott the course was in a very wet cutting, which meant a detour for a short distance. An overgrown straight came next, and after a curve the underbridge below Knightacott was gone, whilst in the valley below Southacott an embankment was followed by 'a very deep and overgrown wet cutting', which meant another detour.

Beyond an overbridge the line became drier and continued so under a second bridge to reach Bratton Fleming station. It was very overgrown with 'wire fence and chickens'!

Regaining the route below the station, the formation ran in quite good conditions through rhododendrons, then the track gradually narrowed until three heaps of rubble (the remains of Lancey Brook Viaduct) were reached. Beyond this, a length was apparently used as a cart track to Chumhill, before an overgrown embankment brought the line under the main road and down through the woods to Chelfham station. Here were two station name boards, lying on the site of the track by the Barnstaple platform. The sleeper marks were clearly visible, as was the stop block of the short siding, together with a gradient post at the beginning of the viaduct. The viaduct was railed off, so there was no alternative but to climb down the path from the Lynton platform to the main road.

I followed the main road to the site of the diversion at Skew Bridge, where I crossed the bridge carrying the minor road over the line (Collard Bridge?) and the river, and then was able to follow the route again until coach No. 6993 appeared ahead. The coach had been repainted green with a white roof and the couplings and brake gear had been removed and dumped in a heap nearby. The interior partitions had been removed and an Elsan closet installed!

Snapper Halt was only a short distance away, and here still stood the truncated coach No. 6991, alongside a garage built on the course of the Barnstaple side.

Having scrambled this far, I felt the remainder of the walk would be best done on the main road and so left the route at this point. During the walk I had seen 'occasional gradient and numbered bridge posts in concrete' along the route.

Such was the scene some eight years after the closure of the line and, except for the demolition of several bridges for road improvements and wartime exercises, the part of the route which I saw that day was largely intact, although, of course, overgrown in many places.

[*Lynton & Barnstaple Railway Magazine*, No. 35, Autumn 1991, pp 12-14.]

"Over the level crossings we went."

A Schoolboy's Trip over the Lynton & Barnstaple Railway*

C. Pennicott

Picture for yourself one of those rare days in Spring with a sun smiling benevolently from a blue, cloudless sky, streets coated with dust, and a broad muddy river flowing turbidly down to the sea.

It was on such a day that I made my journey to Lynton by the 'toy railway'. I leaned from the window of the compartment I had secured, and waited for the train to start. I had not long to wait and in a few minutes we were streaming out of the town station. Over the level crossings we went, for few impatient cars and cycles kept back for us to pass, past the mill, water pouring over the fall, in a cascade, and on to the open fields, with the town behind us.

On my left was a sparkling stream meandering lazily through green pastures, in which lambs gambled, their tails swinging to and fro and where staid old milk cows, ceaselessly chewing the cud, looked up with mildly inquisitive eyes, and then resumed their usual attitude of complete indifference. Through a wood we went, the sun dancing in and out the tall pine trees, the birds twittering and flying from branch to branch.

Then there came a sudden slowing and with a jolt and a clickclicketty-clack we were over the viaduct and into Snapper Halt. No sooner had we stopped than we started again. [Headmaster's Note: The viaduct is at Chelfham, not Snapper.]

But what had happened? A minute ago the sun had been shining and the birds singing, and now - now.

The black clouds climbed up and covered the sun, like someone extinguishing a bright light, and I felt a drop of rain on the tip of my nose. I withdrew my head and let the window drop with a bang. I leaned back in my seat and reflected. How strange it was that the weather should change so quickly! A moment ago the heat had been almost stifling, and now . . .

I watched the rain run in little rivulets down the window. After all, I realised, it was April.

On it came. Rain, rain, rain; it seemed endless. We passed two or three stations before it stopped. With a sigh of relief I turned away from the two farmers who had been discussing the crops and Fat Stock Prices, and once more took up my place at the window. We were passing through a typical cutting of red rock, which seemingly towered above us on either side, and shut out the sun. But it was soon passed and we were once more in open country. Here was another little group of workmen, more cows, more sheep, more green fields, and still more green fields, and yet for all this sameness I sensed an underlying charm in it all.

* The letter was headed by the following introduction: 'The contemplated closing of the Barnstaple and Lynton Light Railway has aroused much interest and caused a certain amount of regret in the West Country. One gentleman, a frequent user of the line, who modestly hides under the title of 'Friend of the Southern Railway', recently was permitted by the Headmaster of Barnstaple Grammar School to offer prizes to the boys for best essays on 'A Trip by rail made during the Easter Holidays from Barnstaple to Lynton'. We have pleasure in printing below one of the prize winning essays, written by Master C. Pennicott (aged 13).'

"Shut that there winder you young rip!"

Then suddenly, and with no warning at all we puffed under a bridge. Clouds of black smoke drifted in and almost choked me. From behind came a chorus of grunts, sneezes and coughs, and a violent expostulation of, 'Shut that there winder you young rip'. I obediently did as I was told and the smoke soon cleared. I must admit that I thought afterwards that if the smoke was half as bad as that which issued from the old farmer's pipe we should all have been dead and gone long ago.

However, that was neither here nor there, and by the time we had entered Blackmoor Gate, all thoughts of it had passed out of my mind. Soon we were off again and passing through lovely scenery to Parracombe. Over a high embankment, over a 'cow creep' and past muddy hedges we chugged, and the sun shone on the white-washed walls of a little farm, with a thatched roof and a tall chimney. Then through pasture and meadow, past copse and stream and into Parracombe. ·

Here on my right, I could see the old grey church, and to my left, down in the valley the more modern one. Here we endured a long halt and I must have dropped off to sleep for I remember no more until we reached Woody Bay, where several passengers, including the grumpy farmer with his evil smelling briar, got off.

On went the train, and soon I was able to see the commons of Woolhanger and West Ilkerton stretching away in the distance. We did not stop at Caffyn's Halt (for the golf course) as there was no one to drop and apparently no one to pick up. Then through wooded hillside, round bends and into the station of Lynton. From here one can see the blue waters of the Bristol Channel in the distance, shimmering in the bright sunlight.

And thus, somewhat changing the poet's words, came 'the end of a perfect journey'.

[*Southern Railway Magazine*, July 1935, page 259.]

LYNTON & LYNMOUTH

THE LYNTON & BARNSTAPLE RAILWAY affords direct communication with Lynton and Lynmouth *via* Barnstaple, which has a direct service of fast trains to and from the Great Western and London and South-Western systems.

The Railway runs through nearly twenty miles of most beautiful Scenery, and from the elevation of the line, the surrounding Country can be viewed to the very best advantage,

---

For Time Tables, etc., send two stamps,

GENERAL MANAGER,

Lynton and Barnstaple Railway,

BARNSTAPLE.

Telephone : Barnstaple 117.

Waterloo to Lynton - 1935

Hamilton Ellis

It was the last week in the life of the Lynton & Barnstaple Railway. My wife said: 'What? You've never seen it?'

I looked sheepish, and a tug going down the Chelsea Reach hooted its disgust.

The people in the Waterloo station inquiry office looked bored when I told them I wanted to make such a trip. Yes, there was a night train, but they did not encourage passengers. Technically this did not become a passenger train until it reached Salisbury. Cheap day trips? Certainly not!

So I went to Paddington.

The inquiries clerk of the Great Western Railway was a lady, in every sense of the term. She said: 'You *must* see the Lynton & Barnstaple! No, we haven't got an excursion running to Barnstaple, but we have one to Plymouth, leaving at midnight. Get a special cheap-day to Taunton, and when you get there, you can get a market-day cheap return to Barnstaple.'

So, late at night, we were at Paddington again, and it was a lively place. Drinking coffee, we met a spruce traveller in shirts, disconsolate because he had missed the 9.50 to the West. We told him that if he came on the excursion he would gain on the train he had missed. He gave me a black cheroot with a straw mouthpiece and rushed off on some late night mission in high spirits. I smoked his gift, we finished up the coffee, spent a happy time looking at the engines, and joined our train. Competently headed by a 'Castle', it was a uniform Great Western express of the period save, as usual, for the odd vehicle. It was an old gaslit clerestory composite, all reserved for a party going to Taunton. The luggage compartment was sealed; I squinted inside and then held my peace. We found two corners elsewhere and watched the other passengers. The large party arrived, with hampers. They walked and talked gravely, and gravely black were their clothes.

My wife said: 'Why, it's a funeral!'

There was nothing else funereal about the train. It got away smartly, and we were fairly comfortable, with two men in the other corners. Somewhere west of Reading I saw that my better half had her feet up. One's wife asleep always makes a pretty picture. Mine was vigorously kicking her neighbour in the fleshy part of the thigh. Her face was placidly serene. She was using both feet.

Taunton is not like Crewe, which is wide awake all night. The train drops you out there in the small hours, as one might imagine a space-ship dumping explorers on some dark and dead asteroid. But we met our traveller in shirts, who had had a lively night with six other people and a small baby with a fine tenor voice, he told us. The funeral party were there, of course, and theirs must have been good hampers, for everyone seemed very jolly indeed, smiling and slapping each other on the back in the dim subway, like mourners in the 'Tarpaulin Jacket'. All the same, we were glad to take leave of them. Sailors are inclined to be sulky about coffins on a ship, and we felt the same way on trains.

Taunton's clerk issued our market tickets as if he were pleased to see us. The Great Western was ever like that; frequently preposterous, especially on its branches, but always amiable. We found an empty two-coach train up in the

---"over the viaduct into delightful Chelfham, and as we clicked over the railjoints the wheels seemed cheerfully to be singing — As of yore--Evermore- As of yore--- Evermore ! "

"OH, THAT 'TWERE POSSIBLE !"

bay, headed by a darkly looming 0-6-0 goods engine, and staked our claims with our rugs and pillows. In the black hour before the dawn, the 9.50 from Paddington came in, after its leisurely wanderings about Bath, Bristol and Bridgwater. When it had thudded away into the darkness, headed by a 'Hall' and a 'Castle' as it faced the climb to Whiteball, we stretched out and turned in. We slept indeed, for it seemed but a moment later that we were cruelly shaken by a bumpy stop and found ourselves in the Great Western station at Barnstaple. A 2-6-2 tank engine came on the other end, and we slid down to the junction, where the Southern Railway seemed to be stretching itself after a peaceful night. Dawn had just broken. A Drummond tank engine simmered cheerily, as they always do, but her neighbour, a Woolwich 'Mogul', looked tired and ashen. She must have had something to do with the 'Tavy'. So we came to Barnstaple Town, and bid good-bye to our Great Western train. We were the only passengers, and I hope the Great Western got its pillows back. We left them headed for Ilfracombe.

There is a difference - or was then - between an independent railway which has became the victim of circumstances, and one which has formed part of a big system. The former become ever more senile and decrepit, while the latter was usually sprightly to the end. This morning the Lynton & Barnstaple did not at first look sprightly, though it was not decrepit. Two very small narrow-gauge coaches, alone without their engine at autumnal daybreak, look rather forlorn, and certainly, as we took our places, the compartments seemed peculiarly narrow and hard, bringing home to us the fact that a passenger railway cannot live by quaintness alone. But the little carriages seemed to warm, and even to swell, as the London newspapers were loaded aboard them, and when *Yeo* backed on, the train was truly alive. Just now, there had simple been empty carriages, of ancient and diminutive sort. Now there was - 'The Newspaper Train!'. *Yeo's* crowned chimney soared proudly above her squat front end; her big round dome shone with polish lovingly bestowed. In the leading coach the first-class smoker, all magnificent with buttoned-in-leather, seemed to be awaiting a nabob or at least a magnate.

Alas, it went on waiting; we were still the only passengers as that strange little train leapt into motion, abruptly as a buck rabbit, and scuttled round the curve to the riverside. *Lew*, the new engine built for the Southern Railway in 1925, was outside the shed at Pilton. This, and the *Yeo* which had hauled the first train on May 10th, 1898, were fated to haul the last one together, a few days hence (September 29th, 1935). I am glad we did not wait for that. How vain and futile are those ceremonial last journeys, when a town turns out with its brass band to take a farewell ride on the train it has neglected for years, and all goes off with volleys of fog signals!

Now we bucketed up the valley as normally and as noisily as if the train had another half-century ahead of it, the engine shouting her *aubade* to the rising sun, the carriages rolling merrily on their 1 ft. 11½ ins. gauge. We swung round the sharp curve and over the viaduct into delightful Chelfham, and as we clicked over the railjoints the wheels seemed cheerfully to be singing 'As of yore - Evermore - As of yore - Evermore!' Oh, that 'twere possible!

At each station, the London papers were dumped out. Who would carry

Goodbye Little Railway,
The Children of Shallowford
loved you...

them next week, and how much later would they be for some people? Who knew? At Bratton Fleming, where the station building crouched under a rock, we crossed the 7.3 out of Lynton, with *Exe* going bunker-first, immediately followed by a first-class observation car, likewise back-to-front. On we went, through the rock cutting and over the shoulder of Exmoor, with *Yeo* spurning her nine miles at 1 in 50 as if she would cross the Andes, given time. The train seemed never to go very slowly; one of the attractions of the very narrow gauge was that, being so near the rocks and the ground, you seemed always to be going much faster than in fact you were. So, breakfasting out of basket on more ham than one dared think of in later years, we came to Woody Bay, and the summit of the line, 1,000 ft above sea level. It was indeed the summit of all the Southern Railway system, being higher than that anonymous spot between Meldon Junction and Bridestowe. (It must be about Aliceford.) Thereafter the train slid, more gently, it seemed, than it climbed, down to the terminus of Lynton, where it sat, still perched high above the ordinary world, on a haunch of the great hills.

We had the morning to play with. It was a pleasant place, especially when treated as a sort of helter-skelter. You simply kept on going down, one way or another, and when you wanted to get back there was always the Cliff Railway, that soaring funicular which is now the Two Towns' only railway. It had turned into a beautiful warm autumnal day, and so it was when we made the return to 'Barum'. This, indeed, was the more pleasant ride of the two. The train was well filled with late holidaymakers; nothing suggested that the railway was about to receive its kiss of death from Waterloo, and the afternoon sunshine on the wooded combes about Chelfham made them very lovely. This time we rode in a compartment with completely open sides above the waist, with four wooden seats, one in each corner, and it was a good thing to remember about this delightful railway which I had never seen before, and would never see again. Near Snapper Halt we stopped while the driver of *Exe*, humanely eschewing the use of his cowcatcher, persuaded some pigs to remove themselves from the track.

All the engines were out except *Lyn*, the Baldwin 2-4-2 tank which was the last survivor of the American engines sent to the British Isles during the great locomotive shortage of the late 'nineties. We found her in the tiny erecting shop where she had first been assembled from her crated components, long ago in 1898. She was never in service again; they were to take her out and break her up with *Exe, Taw* and *Yeo*, the three Manning, Wardle 2-6-2 tank engines of 1898. Only *Lew* survived, to go to a coffee plantation in Brazil, after working the demolition train. The planter said he would have bought the others had he known of them.

Many people came to bid farewell to the Lynton & Barnstaple Railway. There was John Dorling, who wrote its obituary article* and who, I discovered, had been a student with my father in Cologne and Bonn, over 50 years before. There was Henry Williamson, who lived thereabouts, writing *Salar the Salmon*, and who brought his children. 'Good-bye, little railway!' he wrote afterwards. 'The Children of Shallowford loved you!'†

---

*See page 75.
†*The Children of Shallowford* (Faber & Faber), Revised 1939.

So did we; so did I, who saw it only that once. We discouraged melancholy with a good, stuffy Devonshire high tea. The Great Western received us with its usual courtesy; when I grumbled at the two-coach non-corridor train which was to take us back to Taunton, the guard caused to be added an aged but adequate corridor carriage out of the siding. Then there was Taunton, and an up Plymouth express, headed by a 'Hall' and surprisingly composed of thirty-year-old 'Cornish Riviera' carriages, very warm with plenty of room. We were very tired; apart from a dim awareness of Westbury, we slept solidly to Paddington. When, at the end, Lord Ashfield's bus bumbled down the King's Road, the Chelsea Town Hall clocked showed five minutes to midnight. It had been quite a day.

[*Trains Illustrated*, May 1955, pp 190-192.]

"We discouraged melancholy with a good stuffy Devonshire high tea."

The Children of Shallowford

Henry Williamson

I enjoyed that expedition so much that a few Saturdays later we set out again. It was Margy's fifth birthday and for her treat we planned to go to Lynmouth for the day, where among other things a prominent notice-board said: 'Shelley's Cottage, Bed and Breakfast'.

The miniature railway from Barum to Lynton would soon be closed, for few used it at that time. The journey took twice as long as the omnibus, though the little railway was four times as nice to travel on. The children had never travelled on the train, so it would be their first and last time.

Margaret, John, Windles, his friend Sleeboy, A'Bess, and I stood on the platform at the beginning of our journey and inspected the miniature engine.

'Cor, look at the big funnel,' said John.

'I say, look Sleeboy, it's got a cow-catcher, but I suppose it's for the red deer, and what a huge dome - I bet it takes the driver a long time to polish it every morning,' said Windles, whose job it was every Saturday to shine the brass door handles at home.

Margaret touched my hand. 'Look, Dad, isn't it lovely.' She pointed to a baby in one of the carriages. Her only doll was broken some months ago.

We climbed into the last coach. The whistle blew a high comic note and, by the rattling, fussy noises, we were soon travelling at a great rate. Yet the railings and the walls of the wharfside buildings of Rolle Quay were passing very slowly. I put my feet up on the seat before me, and sighed happily, relaxed.

'Cor, 'er's stopped, 'er's used up all the steam!' cried John, disappointment in his voice, as we stood at Snapper Halt, a few minutes later.

'On the contrary, at any moment 'er may bust,' I said. Certainly the engine was wreathed in what appeared to be an excessive volume of steam. 'But perhaps the driver's only stoking her up for a cup of tea.'

'Don't talk rot, Dad,' scoffed Windles, then seeing my face, 'Is it true?'

'Well, I remember the driver of the French troop train which took us up the line to St Omer in 1914, giving us water to make tea with in our mess tins.'

The next carriage was filled with schoolgirls. 'Let's scare them, by pretending to have a fight,' suggested Windles. So we shouted and banged about. A scream like a bantam cock's came from the engine. Rattle, shake, jig. We were off again; past Chelfham with its high viaduct, and up the valley, leaving the little Yeo steam far below.

'I hope there's lots to eat, I'm hungry, I am,' said John, staring at the rusty, empty chocolate machine on Bratton Fleming station.

The train followed the deep wooded valley of the Yeo, on the up-grade all the way. Through hail and rain the valiant little engine hauled us, past fields, vague and grey and suddenly a brilliant green, everywhere streaming with water. Then an excitement: it stopped. The driver and fireman alighted and walked forward. Heads peered out of windows. The driver returned with a lamb under his arm. Margy purred with sympathy. The lamb was put over the wire fence, to join its frantic ewe.

'Why didn't we use the cow-catcher?' grumbled Windles. 'Instead of stopping the train?'

"The lamb was put over the wire fence, to join
it's frantic ewe"......

'You croo' little boy, you!' cried Margaret, adding, with a quick glance at me: 'It's my birthday party, not yours!'

Just before slowing up for Lynton the rain began to fall heavily and we were glad of our raincoats, brought reluctantly by the children and bundled on the wooden rack over our heads.

We walked down the steep stony track to Lynmouth and after some ginger-beer at an inn at the foot of Sinai Hill, we ate our sandwiches in the shelter of a baker's porch, while the rain lashed down. After a three hours' exploration of the beach in the rain, we took the funicular carriage up the cliff to Lynton and climbed to the station again. The railway company had given me a free pass, and so on the return journey I got into the first-class coach, a luxurious pullman made almost entirely of glass, with dark blue upholstery.

'A proper toff is our father,' remarked Windles. From their carriage came shouts, hoots, whistles, and exhortations to the driver. 'Make her spark!'

We changed about at every halt on the line. So did the children, gleefully trespassing into what John called the 'Vust class'. For ninety minutes they kept up their racket. What vitality!

There were some protests against this miniature railway line being closed. Indeed, Lynton Urban District Council sent a delegation to the Southern Railway Company, with a petition to be presented to the management, who had travelled specially from London to Barum to receive it. The management waited at the town station, on the platform, to receive the delegation from the Urban District Council. But when the train came in, it was empty. Every member of the delegation, to save time, had come to Barum by motor car.

Good-bye, little railway. The children of Shallowford loved you.

[*The Children of Shallowford*, (Faber & Faber), Revised 1939.]

Lynton Railway Surprise

Will the Barnstaple to Lynton Railway be finally closed on Sunday? That is the question which is being asked with a roguish grin all over North Devon. After the manner of Geneva there has been an eleventh hour development, and now curiosity is canvassing possibilities. Curiosity is asking, too, who was the mystery man at the other end of the telephone who told the Clerk to the Lynton Urban Council a thing or two about the Lynton and Barnstaple Railway Act of 1895. Apparently there is in North Devon a legal Lawrence of Arabia freelancing to the discomfiture of the Southern Railway. There should be good fun in store.

A Legal Dilemma

What now transpires is that under the Act - as distinct from the Southern Railway Act of 1923, under which the line was transferred - an obligation rests to run the railway for ever and ever apparently irrespective of whether it pays its way. The Act, so the voice whispered over the telephone, lays down that Woody Bay Station must be kept open in perpetuity for passenger and goods traffic, and 'efficiently maintained'. It seems as if some farsighted person back in the nineties looked farther than his nose. North Devon is now preserving that mandatory clause as a poser for the Railway Company, and there is a feeling at Lynton that it might be worth while also to consult counsel so as to be able to check the correctness of the Company's answer.

What About That Half Inch?

Incidentally, there is also another mandatory clause which specifies that the line 'shall be constructed and maintained as a 2 ft gauge'. Now it may be splitting hairs, but in an official statement issued by the Southern Railway last month, announcing the closure, it was stated that 'the gauge of the line is only 1 ft 11½ in.' It may occur to some wag in North Devon presently to insist not only upon the line being kept open, but also upon this little matter of half an inch being put right. That might mean rebuilding the entire line, if in fact the half inch is really missing. There is scope here for real comedy for legal minds, and Lynton should be able to get quite a lot of publicity out of it. Councillors should be getting out their two foot rules.

[*Exeter Express & Echo*, Friday, 27th September, 1935.]

Farewell to Lynton-Barnstaple Railway

There was much more than a tinge of regret about scenes which yesterday marked the passing of the Lynton and Barnstaple Railway. It is true that the railway has not of late years been supported to the extent of making it a paying proposition, but it is evident that the people of the district which it has served for nearly forty years have an attachment for the little railway, and will miss seeing its quaint little trains going to and fro, to say nothing of the regret to those who have been regular users of it.

Whilst there was no official ceremony of any sort to mark the closing of the line, divisional representatives of the Southern Railway travelled on the last train that yesterday ran over the line. It was a cheap half-day excursion, filled to capacity of nine coaches, to draw which necessitated two engines.

Scores of photographs and cinematograph records were taken of the animated scenes on the platform as the last train left, and at many points on the journey to Lynton. At the doors and windows of every house abutting the railway out of Barnstaple, men, women and children waved greetings, and at the various stations *en route* there were groups who had come to see the last train pass.

Even in the fields, shepherds tending their Exmoor flocks paused to give a hand-wave, and at one point a farmer held up a horse-shoe.

The guard of the train wore a sprig of rosemary, which had been presented him as a token of remembrance from one who recalled the early days of the railway.

The Chairman of the Council, and many other people, were at the station at Lynton in the morning to witness the train's arrival. It had received almost as memorable a send-off from Barnstaple as the first train had been given nearly forty years ago.

There was something eerie about the last journey to Barnstaple. As the train moved out of Lynton station, the Lynton and Lynmouth Town Band played 'Auld Lang Syne' to the accompaniment of cheering, the shrieking of the whistles of the engines, and the exploding of detonators on the line. The 'Last Post' was also sounded.

The Chairman of Lynton Council (Mr S.C. Willshere) was cheered with several other members, and they, with the band and about thirty people, accompanied the train as far as Blackmoor Gate in order to have the last ride. Lynton's farewell was, therefore, really given at Blackmoor, where also the little station was crowded to capacity. The darkness of the night was lit up by the head-lights of motor cars, which formed a sort of escort for the train as far as Blackmoor Gate. The roadway runs close to the railway along this part of the route. At every station detonators were exploded, and the train cheered out by villagers, many of whom travelled for miles to take part in the countryside's farewell.

The train reached Barnstaple at 9.45 pm, where, in spite of the rain, a crowd of about 1,000 people waited in the precincts of the station to witness the train come in for the last time. As the passengers left their coaches they did so regretful of the fact that never again would they be able to enjoy riding over those nearly twenty miles of twisting, turning railway, which provided some of the most picturesque scenery in the county.

[*Exeter Express and Echo*, 30th September, 1935.]

Letter to the Editor of the
Western Morning News

'Invicta'

As a frequent visitor to Devon and Cornwall, and being particularly interested in the Lynton and Barnstaple Railway, I was indeed sorry to learn that it has been decided to dismantle what has doubtless been the most picturesque and interesting railway in England.

From my own knowledge a large number of people (many friends acted on my advice) made special journeys to travel on the Lynton and Barnstaple Railway for the sake of the railway itself and the grand scenery *en route*.

Although the date of the sale is now so close, yet there may be time for some business people to get together and buy the whole system outright with a view to maintaining it in its working condition. If representatives of several towns could band together to defray any loss occasioned by such working, one of the greatest attractions of the western counties would be preserved. So much is said and done nowadays to add to the attractions and 'amenities' of various resorts with a view to increasing the number of visitors that it seems a great pity to do away with a most decided and important attraction already in existence.

Certainly the Southern Railway cannot be blamed for discontinuing an unprofitable undertaking, but surely there must be some public-spirited West Country men who could get together to either subsidise the Southern Railway Company or to continue to run the Lynton and Barnstaple Railway as a separate concern. It was with regret that several of us heard that the Bideford and Westward Ho! Railway was done away with. That was a misfortune, but the dismantling of the Lynton and Barnstaple Railway would amount to almost a tragedy.

[*Western Morning News*, 14th November, 1935.]

The Toy Railway's 'Goodbye'

When the Lynton to Barnstaple Toy Railway changed hands twelve years ago it fetched the very respectable sum of £38,000. Yesterday it was put up in lots, and, in a manner of speaking, sold for a song, the five locomotives being knocked down at prices which many people pay for a radiogram.

Next summer visitors to North Devon will miss this little railway, which for so long has lent character to the district it served. Never again will motorists and char-a-banc parties be able to enjoy the novel sight which entertained so many in the past, and for certain there will be fewer smiles in North Devon because of the passing of this quaint little line, soon to be scattered who knows where. But the toy railway will be talked of for a long time to come, and in many homes and gardens - where the old carriages are to get a new lease of life as huts and summer-houses - there will be reminders of it. Never before has an entire railway been sold like this, lock, stock and barrel, in this country. So in a sense history was made yesterday in Barnstaple.

[*Exeter Express and Echo*, 14th November, 1935.]

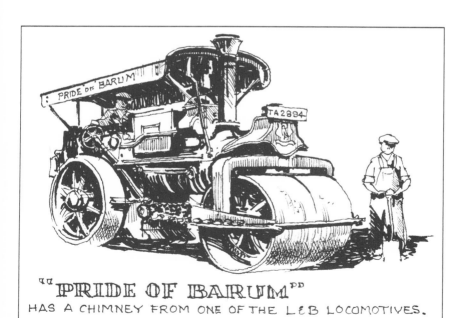

"PRIDE OF BARUM"
HAS A CHIMNEY FROM ONE OF THE L&B LOCOMOTIVES.

"But the toy railway will be talked of for a long time to come, and in many homes and gardens --- where the old carriages are to get a new lease of life <u>as huts</u> and <u>summer houses</u> THERE WILL BE REMINDERS OF IT ....

Yeo - A Memory

Frank E. Box

It is now over eleven years since the residents of North Devon - I could then count myself as one - were startled and dismayed to learn of the impending closure, in the following autumn, of the little line which for thirty-seven years had linked Lynton with the outside world.

Fronting me on my study wall, as I pen these lines, are two brass plates, 'Southern Railway No. E759' and 'Manning, Wardle & Co. No. 1361'. These were once borne by the little engine *Yeo*, the first to be supplied by the Leeds firm to the narrow gauge Lynton & Barnstaple Railway.

It was *Yeo* that provided me with my first trip over the little railway, and seventeen years later, it was on her footplate that I accompanied her on what was her last journey - on the demolition train - before she was broken up; it was also my last trip, of some hundred or so, on the L&BR. It is perhaps fitting, therefore, that this tribute to *Yeo* and her sisters should be penned by me.

It was not until the very end of the nineteenth century that the endeavours, which for twenty years had been made to establish railway communication between Lynton and Barnstaple, through wild and formidable - from an engineering point of view - Exmoor country, culminated, with much rejoicing, in the opening of the line in 1898. On 14th March of that year, for the first time, a locomotive, probably *Yeo*, with one coach, ran through to Lynton. Two days later, a trial trip, with press representatives, was run; it is on record that *Yeo*, the engine used, accomplished the journey in 1 hr 35 mins., the return trip taking 10 minutes longer.

The opening ceremony celebrations took place on Wednesday, 11th May, 1898. The official instructions for the day, a copy of which was lent to me by the late Charles E. Drewitt, General Manager of the line, directed that an engine with driver Milne, was to leave Pilton Yard at 11 am and proceed to Martinhoe (i.e. Wooda Bay, as the station's name was first spelt) to await the passing of the two specials; this was presumably a precautionary measure in the event of a breakdown. The special trains were timed as under:

Train No. 1.

Engine and Carriages, Nos. 6, 4 and 2.

Barnstaple Town	11.15 am
Chelfham	11.40 am
Bratton Fleming	11.55-12.05 pm
Blackmoor	12.25 pm
Wooda Bay	12.44 pm
Lynton	1.00 pm

Train No. 2

Engine and Carriages, Nos. 5, 3 and 1.
Guard Pargeter, driver Pilkington.

Barnstaple Town	11.40 am
Chelfham	12.01 pm
Bratton Fleming	12.25 pm
Blackmoor	12.45 pm
Wooda Bay	1.05 pm
Lynton	1.20 pm

From a photograph of the opening it would appear that *Yeo* had the honour of drawing train No. 1, which was held at Bratton for the presentation of an illuminated address to Sir George Newnes, the Chairman, who had been largely instrumental in the establishment of the railway; it was also stopped outside Lynton to allow Lady Newnes to alight and perform the pretty ceremony of cutting the gaily coloured ribbons stretched across the track. The engine finally steamed into the terminus at 1.17 pm, having taken 1 hr 57 mins., of which stops occupied twenty-six minutes. The line was opened for general traffic on the following Monday, 16th May, 1898, and continued to render useful service until 29th September, 1935.

It was a happy inspiration that suggested the three-letter names of Devon rivers, Yeo, Exe and Taw, for the three original engines. *Yeo* itself seemed particularly suitable as the railway for the first five miles or so of its course closely followed the small river of that name. An additional engine, the Baldwin 4-coupled double-ender, *Lyn*, was soon acquired from the United States' firm to assist in the traffic and, much later, after the line had passed to the Southern Company, Manning, Wardle & Co. supplied another 2-6-2 tank, *Lew*, similar to *Yeo* and her sisters.

Except for passing glimpses from the Ilfracombe train some eleven years earlier, my first acquaintance with the L&BR - and with *Yeo* - was in the late summer of 1918, when the First World War was drawing to its close. The line was still an independent one and was managing to pay its way, the shareholders receiving a small dividend of ten shillings per cent. We had left Waterloo, one August Saturday by the heavily laden 10.50 am express - there were queues at termini and overcrowded trains in those days - which delivered us at Barnstaple Town about three-quarters of an hour late. There, patiently waiting on the 4.30 pm four-coach train for the arrival of her bigger relative, was little *Yeo*. It was 5.17½ pm before we began the first journey over the line which I was to become so familiar, and, owing to crossing and shunting delays, the clock at Lynton showed 6.51 pm (due 5.57 pm) when we eventually arrived; in fairness it should be stated that this was, by a wide margin, the maximum lateness I ever experienced. Our running time for the 19½ miles was, however, only 78 minutes. Thus, somewhat inauspiciously perhaps, began that series of runs which I subsequently recorded between 1918 and 1933. The table set out (below) tabulates the results of all my terminus to terminus trips by unassisted engines during that period.

Down Journeys

Engines	No. of trips down journeys	Averages			Fastest Times	
		Overall Time	Running Time	Load (Tare)	Overall	Running
Yeo	10	88m. 38s.	74m. 04s.	31.2t.	82m. 30s.	68m. 56s.
Exe	10	87m. 39s.	74m. 36s.	29.6t.	74m. 23s.*	65m. 01s.*
Taw	7	86m. 46s.	73m. 28s.	27.9t.	74m. 38s.*	66m. 31s.*
Lew	4	88m. 16s.	74m. 37s.	25.1t.	86m. 42s.	73m. 45s.
Lyn	1	90m. 19s.	74m. 10s.	28.5t.	90m. 19s.	74m. 10s.
All journeys	32	87m. 57s.	74m. 10s.	29.3t.		

Up Journeys

Engines	No. of trips up journeys	Averages			Fastest Times	
		Overall Time	Running Time	Load (Tare)	Overall	Running
Yeo	11	88m. 29s.	74m. 27s.	27.1t.	84m. 44s.	70m. 46s.
Exe	6	85m. 39s.	72m. 59s.	29.3t.	80m. 26s.	68m. 13s.*
Taw	7	88m. 03s.	73m. 53s.	25.1t.	78m. 37s.*	70m. 08s.
Lew	6	88m. 27s.	72m. 40s.	26.8t.	85m. 16s.*	70m. 37s.*
Lyn	3	86m. 05s.	73m. 10s.	30.8t.	84m. 10s.	71m. 30s.
All journeys	33	87m. 39s.	73m. 37s.	27.5t.		

* These trains were recorded with loads of two coaches only - 17¾ tons.

Note: Taking the 1931 working timetable as standard - there was little variation from year to year - the allowances for both down and up trains were practically the same, and averaged 91 minutes overall, and 83 minutes running time. The 7.00 am down 'Newspaper' had the fastest booking, viz., 84 minutes overall and 80 minutes running.

Looking back, perhaps the best remembered feature of the line was its essential friendliness and, if in this article the first person singular has been used mayhap too much, I would crave pardon. It has, however, been done deliberately, as after one or two attempts to 'put over' by an impersonal account the feelings of affection which the line engendered among its patrons, these attempts have been reluctantly 'scrapped', especially after the Editor had intimated that some personal reflections might be preferable. I have, however, no untoward or exciting incidents to recall; there was no serious mishap during the whole period of the railway's existence.

After months of absence one would return to North Devon sure of a warm welcome from the staff, and when at length one's lifework in the city ended, what was more natural than that a cottage, within sound at least of Yeo's shrill but cheerful whistle, should be sought for, found and possession taken? Alas! little was it thought that within two years the Yeo valley would no longer resound to the tones of that whistle.

It was a line of little things - it seemed a marvel how, on a gauge of only 1 ft 11½ in., a coach, 6 ft wide and seating four-a-side, could be safely poised. As one jogged along there was ample time to observe the simple everyday scenes of the countryside; the litter of pigs and the primroses near Snapper; magpies

In the late Spring of 1935,
Exe emerged from the shops at Pilton
after an overhaul, in all the glory of
new paint and glistening brass.

slowly winging their flight from copse to copse; the morning newspaper flung out by the guard as one climbed upwards by the farm at Chumhill; the wild daffodils and some beautiful velvety-coated cart-horse foals below Wistlandpound - lovely name, that white-walled homestead perched so prominently above a sensational horseshoe curve; rabbits in their hundreds on a sunny hillside near Parracombe - in one place there was a colony of black ones. Then perchance the train would stop suddenly while the late driver Frank Northcombe alighted and tenderly lifted into safety a small lamb, which had strayed onto the 'two-foot'.

One memory is of my burglarious exit from my own house, descending the stairs at 5 am in stockinged feet to avoid waking the household, and leaving a laconic note, 'Gone to Lynton, back at 9 am - save some breakfast', to catch the 5.33 am mail from Barnstaple. With *Yeo* at the head of two coaches and two bogie vans, 29½ tons, we were away on time, but had proceeded no further than Pilton crossing when we were held for some 11 minutes, while the signalman made vain efforts to call his colleague at Chelfham. The latter had evidently overslept, and I wonder whether the Pilton Bridge - Chelfham tablet eventually released is the identical one now adorning my wall! However, driver Bray and *Yeo* saved the situation and, with running time from Barnstaple only 66 mins. 56 secs., His Majesty's mails were delivered at Lynton station within three minutes of time. Ten minutes later, on the 7.13 am, *Yeo* was off again on her return trip and landed me back in Barnstaple at 8.38 am (due 8.41), so I was able to keep my breakfast-time appointment. We had again stopped by signal at Pilton, and had made the out and home journey of 38 miles from and to that point in two hrs 49 mins. (13. 5 mph); the actual time during which we were in motion was just under 2 hrs 15 mins., or 16.9 mph, good going over the long and severe gradients of 1 in 50 and over the 1,000 ft summit at Wooda Bay.

Referring to the table, the consistency with which each engine improved on both the over-all and the running times is evident, as is also the fact that, in spite of the difference in level of about 700 ft between the termini the mainly ascending down trains were on the average only about half a minute slower than the descending up ones. The down trains, after a nearly level start from Barnstaple for about 1½ miles, were confronted with over 12 miles of adverse grades, mostly at 1 in 50, broken only by a 2 mile descent between Blackmoor and Parracombe, before reaching the summit at Wooda Bay; the up trains had about 5 miles, mainly at 1 in 50 to surmount between Lynton and Blackmoor.

Yet again, on its final run on Saturday, 28th September, 1935, did I travel by the mail, and again it was *Yeo*, with driver Wallace Worth, which hauled the heavily laden train, for behind the two coaches was a tail of two loaded bogie coal wagons, our gross load being over 45 tons. As she toiled upward over the slippery rail *Yeo* illuminated the darkness with a fine display of sparks. At the several stations postal officials were in waiting to receive for the last time the railborne mails for the still sleeping villages, and as in the grey dawn we passed the many farmsteads, or '-cotts', their windows brightly lighted, *Yeo* saluted with her whistle, for the last time, the farm folk starting their day's toil. Then, four minutes early, at 6.56 am, the last mail-bags were delivered at Lynton station. Quickly uncoupling, *Yeo* ran round the train to form the 7.15 am up, while, still some seven minutes before sunrise, I essayed to photograph the unloading of the mails. Returning with *Yeo* as far as Blackmoor, I was able to join there the last 'newspaper', the 7 am ex-Barnstaple, with *Lew* at its head, and accompany it back to Lynton, where we arrived about five minutes early, and also to secure the picture of the last rail-carried newspapers.

In the late spring of 1935 *Exe* emerged from the shops at Pilton after an overhaul, in all the glory of new paint and glistening brasswork, thereby raising vain hopes that it could not be intended to close the line in a few months' time.

On the last trip on Sunday, 29th September, 1935, when it fell to *Lew* and *Yeo* to haul the heavily laden nine-coach train with some 300 excursionists to Lynton and back, I would write little. The whole proceedings seemed strangely out of tune with the occasion, being regarded by many as a picnic. This feeling was augmented on the return journey when, in the gathering darkness, the Lynton band accompanied the train as far as Blackmoor. To friends of the railway it was a dismal day indeed, and the steady drizzle through which our two little engines finally brought the train into Barnstaple was more in keeping with the event, as was also the quiet ceremony, when on the following morning Mr Ford, the Barnstaple Town station master, laid a wreath sent by a resident at Wooda Bay on the dead-end at Barnstaple Town.

Prior to the sale on 13th November, the SR removed the track between Lynton and mile-post 15½, and *Yeo* was employed in hauling the demolition train. On 8th November I photographed - in a drizzle - *Yeo* and the demolition gang just after the last section of track had been lifted, and then travelled back to Barnstaple on her footplate with driver Nutt, my last trip and *Yeo's* last duty! Nutt and Northcombe had both started as cleaners at Pilton, when the line was first opened, and had remained in its service during the whole time of its existence. My last photograph of *Yeo* with the fatal marking 'Lot 7' on her bunker, was taken just after her arrival at the transfer siding - her last duty faithfully done. In the background are the trees fringing the little river, after which she was named, near its outfall into the Taw estuary.

Five days later, as 'Lot 7', she was auctioned for £50 as 'scrap'; with the exception of *Lew*, she and her sisters were broken up at Pilton shortly afterwards. *Lew* survived, and on behalf of the contractors continued to work the demolition train during the spring of 1936; she was finally shipped to Brazil, where - it is to be hoped - she is still doing useful service.

Readers who desire to learn more about the railway and its history are referred to Mr L.T. Catchpole's delightful little book, *The Lynton & Barnstaple Railway, 1895-1935.** It contains numerous diagrams and illustrations, and also a gradient profile; logs of the journeys mentioned in this article are included in a short appendix on the locomotive performance.

In concluding this article I would mention that my friend, Mr W.E. Hayward, of Weston-super-Mare, possesses the name and number plates of *Yeo*, together with the nameplates of *Lew* and *Lyn* - the latter still doing useful service as the name plate of his house. It is pleasing to record that the SR have also preserved at Eastleigh a complete set of the five name-plates of the L&BR locomotives.

[*Railway Pictorial*, No. 1, Winter 1946/47, pp 25-30.]

*Still in print, now in its 7th edition, Oakwood Press.

The Lynton and Barnstaple Railway

John W. Dorling

Rarely, if ever before, has the closing of a railway aroused such keen interest as has been awakened throughout the country by the running of the last trains over the narrow gauge Barnstaple-Lynton section of the Southern Railway. This is to be attributed very largely to the unusual character of the line and the magnificent scenery through which it passes.

For quite twenty years prior to its opening there were schemes to secure rail communication between Barnstaple and Lynton, and there had been several Acts authorising various lines. All had come to nothing. Then, largely through the influence of Sir George Newnes the Act of June 27, 1895, incorporating the Lynton and Barnstaple Railway Company 'for the construction of a 2 ft gauge line from Barnstaple to Lynton', came to fruition. Even then there was a rival scheme, under which a line of standard gauge was to be constructed from Lynton via Blackmoor and across the edge of Exmoor, to a junction with the GWR Taunton-Barnstaple line at Filleigh, near South Molton. It seemed strange as one travelled in the little puffing trains to think that, had this line been constructed, one might have travelled to Lynton by a coach off the GWR Cornish Riviera Express. However, the narrow gauge won, and construction was formally begun on September 17, 1895, when Lady Newnes cut the first sod at Shambleway, near Lynbridge. Sir James Szlumper was the Consulting Engineer.

Festivities at Barnstaple in connection with the opening began on May 10, 1898, when a Mayoral at-home in the Music Hall was attended by 400 guests. The formal opening took place on the following morning. The district seems to have made a public holiday of the opening, triumphal arches were erected and towns and villages gaily decorated. After a procession to the North Walk, where the L&B and the LSWR had erected a new joint station (now the Town station) in place of the latter company's Quay station, in use since the opening of the Ilfracombe line in 1874, there were many speeches, and the Mayor of Barnstaple travelled to Lynton. Here the High Sheriff of Devon remarked on the low cost of the line (£5,000 a mile) and Sir George Newnes defended this railway as opposed to another scheme for a line from Minehead to Lynton. A grand display of fireworks, free concerts and dances followed.

Public traffic began on May 16. The line, 19½ miles long, was single track, consisting of flat-bottomed rails spiked direct to transverse sleepers and well ballasted. The actual gauge was 1 ft 11½ in. The original board of directors comprised Sir George Newnes (Chairman), Col. Evan B. Jeure, Sir Thomas Hewitt, and Mr W.H. Halliday, all closely identified with Lynton. The first General Manager was Mr Frank W. Chanter who had been Resident Engineer during the building of the railway; a year after it was opened he was succeeded by Mr. C.E. Drewitt, who held office during the whole of the remaining independent life of the company. The original staff numbered 30.

Early association of the railway with public motor services resulted from efforts to provide easy communication between Lynton and Ilfracombe. At first horse-drawn coaches provided a service between the latter town and Blackmoor station, but early in 1903 Sir George Newnes with characteristic

LYNTON AND BARNSTAPLE RAILWAY

LOCAL SERVICE between BARNSTAPLE AND LYNTON, and vice versa.

All Trains Parliamentary

DOWN		Week Days					Sun.
		am	am	am	pm	pm	am
Barnstaple (Town) dep.		6 35	8 40	11 30	3 45	5 24	7 30
Chelfham		7 1	9 9	11 52	4 8	5 47	7 54
Bratton		7 20	9 25	12 9	4 27	6 3	8 15
Blackmoor		7 45	9 50	12 31	4 49	6 28	8 40
Wooda Bay		8 9	10 11	12 53	5 10	6 49	9 4
Lynton	arr.	8 25	10 28	1 9	5 26	7 5	9 20

UP		Week Days					Sun.
		am	am	pm	pm	pm	pm
Lynton	dep.	6 14	9 10	1 50	3 25	5 45	5 38
Wooda Bay		6 33	9 28	2 8	3 43	6 3	5 57
Blackmoor		6 58	9 53	2 31	4 6	6 28	6 22
Bratton		7 23	10 15	2 53	4 31	6 50	6 47
Chelfham		7 40	10 29	3 8	4 46	7 5	7 4
Barnstaple (Town) arr.		8 2	10 50	3 30	5 7	7 26	7 26

From the original timetable of the Lynton and Barnstaple Railway, issued on the opening to public traffic on May 16th, 1898. The spelling of 'Wooda Bay' will be noticed.

enterprise decided to work motors. He bought two 22-seat, 16 hp Milnes-Daimler motor wagonettes and inaugurated a service in June of that year. A contemporary London newspaper comment said: 'This is the first time that a railway company has started a motorcar service to collect and distribute passenger traffic, and it may be hoped that the example thus set may be followed by some of the great companies'. By a curious coincidence the example was not only quickly followed by the GWR, but the first enterprise of the latter was actually begun with the same vehicles, for the Lynton & Barnstaple Railway found its enterprise unpopular in a district where horse-drawn coaches were at the height of their popularity and, following difficulties with the police as to 'speeding above 8 mph', disposed of the two Milnes-Daimlers to the GWR. It was with these that the latter inaugurated its famous Helston to the Lizard route on August 17, 1903.

The railway started from Barnstaple Town station (LSWR) from a bay platform let into the one platform for the Ilfracombe line, which here is single. On the narrow gauge there was a run-round road, also several sidings alongside the standard gauge ones for transfer of goods. There was also a separate signal box for the Lynton trains. The line throughout was signalled and tablet working was used; the whole length was fully fenced. Within recent years a short length of the line was laid with steel sleepers.

Shortly after leaving the Town station on a sharp curve, two main roads were crossed on the level, and the carriage and wagon sheds at Pilton were passed. There was a well-type turntable here. Open country was soon entered, and following the River Yeo through meadows, Snapper Halt was reached. The platform here as elsewhere, except Barnstaple, was very low, a mere line of bricks marking the edge. A small tin hut did duty as waiting room. Beautifully wooded country followed till Chelfham Viaduct, 4½ miles from Barnstaple, came into view. This, the largest engineering work on the line, is constructed of brick and consists of eight spans, each 42 ft wide and 70 ft above the road below.

Just across the viaduct the train ran into Chelfham Station, the most prettily situated station on the line. It was for all the world as if the train had run into a tunnel of trees; so nearly did they meet overhead. Chelfham was a crossing place, with two platforms; signals and points were worked from a lever frame on the up platform. There were waiting rooms, and also water tanks. Leaving Chelfham the train climbed upwards through densely wooded country to Bratton Fleming, where there was one platform and a short siding. The waiting room, with ivy wreathed walls and moss covered roof, was set against the rock face. A deep rock cutting followed, and the coaches, which overhung the track by at least 2 ft, seemed almost to touch the rocky sides. Once out of the cutting, the line made a serpentine curve around the head of a valley, completely reversing its direction twice, and climbed up to Blackmoor (12 miles from Barnstaple). This station, which was another crossing place, had two sidings, goods sheds, and more pretentious buildings. Onwards to Parracombe the route lay across open moorland country, and at the halt, as at Chelfham, there was a water tank.

More moorland scenery, interspersed with views of the sea between the heather covered hills, followed as the train wound up to Woody Bay. Some of

"Every village turned out to witness the passage of the last train"........

the best station buildings were situated here and an upper quadrant signal was noticed. Woody Bay (or more correctly Wooda Bay, as indeed it was shown in the original timetable, which is reproduced) was the summit of the line, being just 1,000 ft above sea level. Here, as at Blackmoor, some concrete sleepers were noticed. After the train had dipped under the main road for the fifth time, and called at Caffyns Halt (for the Golf Links), it followed the valley of a tributary of the West Lyn. The hillsides are well wooded and at times the train ran along behind a veritable screen of beech trees. The views obtained were magnificent and running into Lynton station the sea could be seen ahead gleaming in the sunshine.

Lynton station was 750 ft above the sea level at Lynmouth and some 200 ft above the main town at Lynton. It consisted of one main platform with a bay and a run-round road. The two main tracks continued beyond the station through a goods shed to a small yard equipped with a crane. There was also a small engine shed.

Since July 1, 1923, the Lynton & Barnstaple Railway has formed part of the Southern Railway, which acquired it under the powers of the Southern Railway Act, 1923, at the price of £31,061 for the railway, plus £7,307 for the 4 tank engines, 17 coaching and 24 merchandise vehicles, and £899 for land and buildings. It should be emphasised that the line was unaffected by 'grouping' and was not acquired under the Railways Act, 1921. The capital of the Lynton & Barnstaple Railway was £85,000 in ordinary shares, and there were loans amounting to £42,400. The latter comprised an original £26,500 in 4 per cent first debentures, and a subsequent £15,900 in 4½ per cent second debentures. Dividends of ½ per cent were paid for each of the years 1913 to 1921 inclusive on the ordinary shares, and the railway was, like the main lines, under Government control during the war period, taking its share of the Government compensation awarded in 1921. Its best year before the war was 1913, when railway gross receipts were £9,668, working expenses £6,640, and net receipts £3,028. In 1922, its last year of separate working, receipts were £14,511, and expenses £14,948, and no dividend was paid on the ordinary shares.

There were five engines on the line. Three 2-6-2 outside cylinder side tanks were the original locomotives supplied for the line by Manning, Wardle & Co. of Leeds in 1897; these were numbered 759, 760 and 761 and named *Yeo, Exe* and *Taw*. A similar engine was built by the same firm for the Southern Railway in 1925 and was named *Lew* (No. 188). The fifth engine was built by the Baldwin Locomotive Works in America, sent over in boxes and assembled at Barnstaple in 1898. It was a 2-4-2 tank, and was No. 762 in the SR lists, and was named *Lyn*. All the engines seem to have worked well; all had very tall chimneys and large brass domes, with low side frames. They were fitted with miniature cowcatchers. The coaches, of which there were 17, were built by the Bristol Carriage & Wagon Co. Ltd. As with the locomotives, they overhung the track by about 2 ft on each side. There were two first class observation saloons glassed in at one end as well as the sides; from these splendid views could be obtained. Some of the vehicles contained a centre compartment, roofed over, but with low open sides, and one seat in each corner; these made very pleasant travelling in the summer. The coaches were lit by acetylene, generators being fitted at the end of each coach. All vehicles were fitted with centre buffers and couplings combined. There was also 24 freight wagons of closed and open types. Since its acquisition by the Southern Railway the equipment has been brought up to date, carriages re-upholstered, and new goods rolling stock provided.

This summer the trains left Barnstaple at 5.33 am (mail), 7 am (newspaper), 10.15 am, 1.33, 3.15, 4.25, and 7.50 pm (Fri. and Sat. only). From Lynton the times were 7.3, 9.25 am, and 12.42, 3.30, 6.7, 8.4 and 9.30 pm (Fri. and Sat. only). In winter the 1.33 and 7.50 from Barnstaple and the 3.30, 8.4 and 9.30 from Lynton were suspended, leaving an effective service of two down and four up trains a day, since the early trains were of little use for passengers. In 1932, an 'express' was run, calling at Blackmoor and Bratton in 80 min. Apart from this, however, the time allowed for the journey, including seven stops was 1 hr 32 min., from Barnstaple to Lynton, mostly on a rising gradient, and a few minutes less on the return journey. The ruling gradient was 1 in 50; there was a stretch of nine miles of this.

The last trains ran over the line on Sunday 29th September, being a half excursion from Barnstaple. Every village turned out to witness the passage of the last train, drawn by *Yeo* and *Lew* (the former drew the first train 37 years ago). In the evening, in the mist and gloom, all Lynton seemed to have turned out to bid farewell to its railway. The Town Band insisted on accompanying the train as far as Blackmoor, and the engines drew their train of nine coaches out of Lynton station for the last time, to the accompaniment of their own shrill whistles, the playing by the band of 'Auld Lang Syne', and the explosion of detonators. On the following day the final touch to the obsequies was paid when the station master at Barnstaple laid on the narrow gauge track a wreath of bronze chrysanthemums sent by Paymaster Captain Woolf, RN (Retd) of Woody Bay, which bore a black-edged card:

To Barnstaple and Lynton Railway, with regret and sorrow from a constant user and admirer, 'Perchance it is not dead, but sleepth.'

This fascinating little line thus finished its career amidst public interest comparable with that which greeted the opening of the railway, when, at the arrival of the first train at Lynton, Lady Newnes severed ribbons across the track amidst the cheers of a crowd which included prominently lifeboatmen wearing their cork jackets. Throughout its career it has kept its record clean by having had no passenger fatality. Its passing leaves Lynton in the position it was 40 years ago, namely, that of being the furthest town in England from a railway.

[The Railway Magazine, November 1935, pp 333-342.]